THE BEST COLLEGE VERSE

1970

LAUREATE

THE
Best College Verse
of 1970

Edited by

HARRIET ELLEN ROSE.

and

THEODORE READE NATHAN

THE LAUREATE PRESS, LTD.
New York

Library of Congress Catalog Card Number 77-142422

PRINTED IN THE UNITED STATES OF AMERICA BY
Theo. Gaus' Sons, Inc., BROOKLYN, N. Y.

In Favor of Excellence . . .

There is more meaning in the restlessness and tension of young people than headlines and demonstrations reveal. Their folksongs and poetry merit being heard today and preserved for tomorrow.

In compiling this anthology, a decision had to be made concerning the degree to which Laureate would reflect the thought and attitudes of young people living in these times and the degree to which it should be limited to poems with true value as poetry. The choice was made in favor of excellence.

The poems in this book were selected from some six thousand submitted. Although no attempt was made to include all areas of the United States or every type of educational institution, good poetry is hardly a matter of geography and several hundred schools in all parts of the country are represented.

Poetry, like education, is the luxury of an advanced form of civilization. It is as little connected with the direct pursuit of survival as are most modern occupations, with the obvious exception of farming and building. The poet, like the scholar, has chosen to devote his life to ideas in a product age.

Unlike scholarship, poetry is not confined to ideas alone, usually best stated in simple prose.

Poetry often includes a myriad of associations impinging on an idea and radiating from it, recreating the rhythm of the mind process. The curricular disciplines undertaken in universities involve the writing of academic papers in which the student seeks to demonstrate by scholarly methods all possible proofs of his theory. The poem, on the other hand, involves an interconnection of ideas and associations stemming from those ideas. The end result evokes what may be termed a vision.

The word alone, however, cannot encompass the total poetic creation. Vision has to do with sight as does the word "image." The poem is basically a sound form. All its images and visions are created by sound patterns which are "seen" in what Wordsworth calls the inner eye. The poem, whether it consists of a single image or a series, is held together by patterns of sound, the rhythm which underlies and intensifies the meaning.

This volume contains poems in all categories from blank verse to formal, highly structured patterns. The standard by which they were chosen is the suitability of rhythm to meaning.

Laureate offers a wide variety of poetic visions. Unlike a poem, it attempts no real unity; but the reader may impose on this collection his total impression of the direction of things to come.

Some of the college poets in these pages have been widely published. For others, it is their first appearance in print. Some will grow to become the poets studied in tomorrow's classrooms. A few may never write anything as worthy again. All, however, have been influenced by the world of today. Some employ ideas unknown to past generations and represent the poetry of the future.

THE EDITORS

Index of Authors

INDEX OF AUTHORS (*continued*)

INDEX OF AUTHORS (*continued*)

INDEX OF AUTHORS (*continued*)

THE BEST COLLEGE VERSE

SEA BLOOD

Who long ago had shuddered on this sand, built fire under
        these same rocks,
This cliff, like a mermaid draped in green and wet seaweed,
glistening in the new light of the sun-star that was young
        and warmer then;
Who caught the early fish with bare hands and tore apart
the useless muscles and what would be blood (what from
        this ocean became blood),
Where now is steady surf and calming rhythm in the heart,
        the useless mind lulled;
Who when lying near the fire, saw strange colors as the
        orange orb would melt
and the sky turn frighted black,
That all became a nightly mermaids' spectacle;
Who shared the tidewaters with horseshoe crabs, primeval
        creatures that had no brain but armor,
That live without blood still, for the sea still gives them life.

by SUSAN C. CAMPBELL, Mount Holyoke College, Mass.

A SCENE

In the black silken lap of Meurtra La Fois
Lies the drooling quiet head of Cornelius, her son,
Whose eyes slowly spin in rhythm
With the gray curls of his dusty hair.
Three bluebirds watch the motionless solitude
And study the angle of his reclining eyes.
A moment ago they chirped a reveille
But only a black crackling fold
Unwound to chase the fly from her knee
Into the monotonous gray humid sky.

by TRICIA KNOLL, Yale University, Conn.

1

DIEGO

The man
watches moondust
filter down an
anise sky, wrap
languidly
around a star,
and vanish.

Morning glimpses
yesterday (bearded)
in the antic mirror,
and still the streets
below stay open,
beckoning.

A girl laughs—
inviting?
Lambent mirror-moment;
Fire's sudden focus
Burns!

(Long ago) now dry
of splintered daybreaks,
he slowly knots his tie
and turns, tusk-bent,
toward noon.

by CAREN GOLDBERG, Hunter College, N. Y.

GENEALOGY

In Madison, the family wrote books
about the summer flowers of Wisconsin;
stretching in meadows, tentative as jonquils,
made sketches of the sapling trees of spring
and diagrams of plants. The Duggars knew
the ways to map the patterns of things growing.

2

They were dependent, then, on something's growing:
The men inscribed, in several heavy books,
their farmers' treatises—the things they knew
about the moss and mushrooms of Wisconsin—
and made their fortunes. The women, in the spring,
gave birth to babies fresh as yellow jonquils.

Their grandfather ministered to boys and jonquils,
bred flowers and restructured men for growing.
Under his kitchen windows in the spring
he planted hybrids, or devoured books
that told him how his sons were, in Wisconsin,
and how their children were, and what they knew—

Their father had not told them, but they knew
their mother was as fragile as the jonquils.
And when the winter rattled through Wisconsin,
killing the fragile things God meant for growing,
the children cried, and curled into their books,
like crocuses come out too soon for spring.

And Madison was tired in the spring—
as any mother grows, the Duggars knew.
The youngest boy had tired of his books;
weary of trees and of the flowering jonquils,
he left the level lowlands for the growing
cities in the states west of Wisconsin,

—and never took his children to Wisconsin
because they all were students in the spring
and had no time to watch the jonquils growing—
wrote careful theses on the things he knew,
and in the city, planted paths of jonquils,
printing dimensions in his weighty books.

His son has learned Wisconsin from the textbooks,
indifferent to spring. But would he love the growing
if he knew his light eyes shone like yellow jonquils?

by AMY SIEGEL, Vassar College, N. Y.

3

REFLECTIONS

A PREMISE

In this gothic library a church-like silence
Arching with cathedral grace transmits me nothing—
Nor would pews and pulpits, choir lofts and altar cloths
Imbue this noiseless emptiness with Grace.

A PSALM

But sometimes moments I own angelic senses.
My eyes, perceive no longer—they are optic instruments
My ears, hear no longer—they are sonic meters
My mind, understands no longer—it is a mirror . . .
  A knot unties inside my belly, then,
Plastic atom after plastic atom my tongueless body
Knows: I am more than just myself.

A POST SCRIPT

"I" was in this poem before anything
How could I avoid it? My person, only I, have known for me.

      by EDWIN H. MARTIN, Harvard University, Mass.

IN TRIBUTE

I painted Picasso today,
on the beach amidst
broken shells and weeds,
the butts of last night's party.
After a heated argument
we watched the sun drown,
overwhelmed by the answer
thanks to the proof of a Prufrock era.

4

We cast our lines coldly,
eyeing fishermen on horses
that gyre on waves to the new moon,
counting 1,2,3, to 13-spear a sphere.
The wind hovers,
and we watch, hiding,
from a stirring achievement.
"That's enough" he said,
and he waited,
while I said goodby.

by DOUGLAS MENAGH, Fairfield University, Conn.

WINDS

Wind whisks a scroll of cigarette smoke back over the shoulder
Of the lone man gazing out to sea, the glimmer of horizons in
    his eye,
And it is January, the month of beginnings;
Wind ruffles a head-feather of the slate-grey junco dauntless in
    the snow,
And it is February, and the kernel of the world is shriveled
    with cold;
Wind tangles like an animal in the wicker snare of bare tree-
    branches,
Deranging the tree-shape in its struggle to be free,
And it is March, and winter falters in the long roar of its
    filibuster;
Wind wrinkles a skein of blue silk sky mirrored in a puddle,
And it is April, and the wheelrut hardens in the drying mud;
Wind shakes the perfume from the great white mane of the
    apple-tree thick with blossoms and bees,
And it is May, drowsy with the drowsiness of lovers;
Wind before the storm flutters the silver-lined leaves of poplar,
Until the whole spire of tree flickers and glistens,
And it is June, purple with thunder;

Wind swells at dawn like breath through the sleep-heavy
    bedroom,
With all the honey of summer trembling in its trail,
And it is July, and the man, waking, brushes with his lips the
    breast of the sleeping woman;
Wind bloats the stiff white of window curtains like sails of a
    schooner,
And it is August, moody with doldrums;
Wind buffs the waxy polish of the wasp-worried apple,
And it is September, the time of great ripeness;
Wind stirs up the fallen red of maple like sediment in the mellow
    amber of day,
And it is October, and all the year's ciders and wines have been
    pressed, and all the grains hoarded;
Wind drives the great grey battalions of drizzle hissing over
    the bristling reeds of the marshes,
And it is November, the month of boredom;
Wind scrapes its unpared nails across the bare glass of ice-
    crusted fields,
And it is December, and there is no one to listen.

by MARTIN GRUBER, Brooklyn College, N. Y.

LUCY

Wispy clouds of balled-up light
           hang
                    suspended
                          in
                                midair,
lifted up by oceans of yellowish breath
        breathed by some hidden dragon.
Leaves crinkle underfoot, reflecting hazy filaments—
              naked now—
          cast away by idle forms.

Streetlights lord over chilled night air
and a single couple wends the way
through pyramids of refugees
sprinkled on the pavement,
helter-skelter
freed.

In this night of chilling fog
two hands reach out
And find their own, locking in
the misty remnants
of evenings past,
meandering
into
a
future
that springs up for wanderers
among the castaways.

by STEPHEN R. LAUERMANN, Drew University, N. J.

The moon is a down
the shadows have stopped
their shaking
even California might go
under from a quaking
The sparrows are cracking
their tiny skulls upon the walls
the cat's meow has crawled
out of his tongue and
curled around his collared neck
and what do you expect
a revolution without a waking?

by BARBARA BEEMAN, Jersey City State College

Gabriel touches the thousand clouded
sky with the sound of his sacred music,
borne aloft upon multi-colored rays
streaming forth, white-hot, from stained glass windows
set high in the vastness of an aged stone
cathedral. Spirit tunes maddeningly
weave their way into our opened minds,
the spell of Nazareth and redemption
settles upon our upturned faces,
and Gabriel plays on, oblivious
to all but the purity of his sound.
We sit, transfixed, in a circle upon
the smooth marbled floor; blue shadows flicker
about our bodies, drawn together
in ecstasy of Gabriel's music.

by MARIANNE C. WILKES, Douglass College, N. J.

FEEL TO MAKE ME FEEL

I dreamt we were on the ceiling
And you had the part of God
And I that of Adam.
Odd?

The painter mixed the colors
Controlled the creation
Decided our fates
With dilettante's delight.

Lying on the cloud,
How quiet was I
Unfulfilled
Listless
Slightly chilled
With weak knees
And limp hand
And heart of ennui.

8

Titanically active
Strongly alive you were
And seemingly
Did you strive
To bridge the gap
To give sustenance to me
And touch me
With your dynamism.
And feel
To make me feel.

The artist lay beneath us
Dabbling in his mind
How to finish.
Considering much
Whether to join
Whether to touch
Our fingers,
When he fell from his ladder.

Awakened
I lay there on my bed
You, over there on yours
With our arms over the sides
Almost together
The fingers a fingertip apart
Soon to press together.

by MICHAEL BOSWORTH, Holy Cross College, Mass.

After the fraudulence of feathers,
the veiny glimmerings in August grass,
we resolved to become more sensible;
walking, we spliced weeds, plaited low boughs,
struck for home while it was still light.
We shut the windows at dark;
the night flung a tentacle across the room,
a lamp pitched figures fluttering on walls.

9

Before the ebb of shadow,
the rustling of branch into light,
we tossed to the foghorns' croak;
each blast hung in the misted air,
spiralling through our conception of time,
folding itself within much-pleated bark.

The dawn pulsed onto our eyelids;
night flickered above the brows.
Darkness did not flow from the sky;
the birds carried it across earth in their beaks,
as night scatters feathers from its jaws.

by JILL ROBBINS, Vassar College, N. Y.

A HUNTER'S MORTALITY

like all faceless faces, he placidly drifted.
somehow, unimportantly, marrying,
casually gliding, no turmoil jagged.
until that dreary dumb-tongued day,
drawn door a slit
that blighted light, now golden bright
as a springtime never seen, never missed.
caressingly a finger had grazed his neck,
and that solitary worm, firm, perched,
nuzzled, ate, and gnawed.
no, now he did not sit in nature temple
breathing the beauty of a fleeting world,
but brutal, dealing in the quick death
of a flat shot nuzzling to hearts home.
his long-lived rage roared red
in retort for the boiling blood
of the animals that seemed always
to live on.

for the king sitting crowned and regal
in his head, he would not let
the fury fail as long as the blood
coursed strong, sure, and silent
veined. he would ceaseless spill.
in him the stream did not flutter weak,
but heart beat dumb forcing maggot seeds
that would honeycomb and hollow
that ever-certain fleeting flesh.
they whispered, "the jeweler
has placed the tumor in its setting
and it blossoms in his body.
it's so terrible we can't speak the word."
but the word was made flesh
and echoed always in festering caverns.
and as that simple growth unfolded,
the brute beast frenzy grew,
and more animals dropped with a thud
after a shot,
until that exquisite brute beast mind
turned the gun and toe hunted out trigger.

by MATTHEW WILSON, La Salle College, Pa.

BUM

The bum on the park bench,
      collector of rare dust,
    smiles at yellow cars
    circling the planet
               in search of parking space.
Bathed in silence,
    pocked with sunlight beneath the gossiping elm,
he needs no window shopped reflection
    to make existence real,

11

Eyes pinched like closed umbrellas,
    cheeks like saddlebags
        heavy with lost love letters,
       he guards the last reviewing stand
      in beauty's blushing pageant
         down
            main
               street,
Hunched with heavy stillness,
    the poet hidden beneath abandoned whiskers,
       stands on his shoulders.
His hand,
       tatooed in parlors of rough wind,
    explores the inside
           of his flannel thigh
    like the sure hand of an old lover.
No one sees him dancing.

by MITCHELL DITKOFF, Brown University, R. I.

THE BOSTON COLD

I could read a book by the night-snow's light
As the fine stuff blew like smoke
Off the bare buildings;
And spring only a matter of days . . .

A seagull harped on the children birds
Only this morning
And I easily came to the time of my job
To shave at the icy mirror
While trucks boxed my ears
Back and forth toward the day's long run
With diesels shifting the goods of the motherlode
Morning up the snowy right-of-way.

Tonight by electric light,
I read the Bible
Where Heaven opened unto John
And he beheld a white horse,
White as paper, white as snow;
But I cannot catch the glimpse at morning
That I cannot pray for in the night.

Out on the snowy battlefield,
A plow blinks into random piles.
The driver smokes. The job's over.
A light pulses in the empty intersection
Of winter and spring creaking
In the wind, shifting in the dreamworld
Whose pillow's a cheek for a weeping willow
And a saddle for a skull full of reins.

The Boston fallen horse of snow
Is stained with dark windows
And rasps with broken gulls and green shovels.

                    by JONATHAN KLIMO, Brown University, R. I.

DEEP WINTERS

In our deep winters we like to hide somewhere
Out beyond the flailing willow branches on the wind—
        naked now,

Out beyond the pond that's been frozen over since November
Where you wonder that powdered snow just takes an imprint
        slightly—then forgets.

You wonder why the crooked logs get frozen half out of the
        water
And how came the bird tracks in the snow when all the birds are
        gone—supposedly.

You wonder why the wind blows colder beyond the southern
knoll
And you wonder how long you can kid yourself into thinking
that you're not thinking about yourself anymore.

It's not for long,

You return and not much damage has been done,
For we all find it imperative to hide sometimes
in our deep winters.

by SISTER MARY JEANNETTE, CSSF
D'Youville College, N. Y.

THE FIELDS

The fields lie empty.
The fields lie still.

In Winter the snow comes.
In Spring the rain.
In Autumn the leaves.

Birds pass.
Deer graze.
Snakes weave silent paths.

An old wagon rusts in a corner.
A stone wall crumbles,
Slowly.

The wind blows,
The leaves stir,
And the fields lie.

by RICHARD HANSON, Manhattan College, N. Y.

EVE'S ABSENCE

cool, dark mossy
   water passing in
through the space between my ribs
depositing green on the bones,
molting to crescent feeling
     lights up the strung pearls
gleaming over the falls

under the wing of the baby duck
is a scooped-out place for feeling
imprint of mother

the cage has a plaster
cast festering underneath
lion pacing, tossing
back her mane, in
a heat

     by DAVID M. KATZ, City College, N. Y.

THE RETURN HOME

One foot down and then the second,
black forms on the screen
silhouetted,
flickering uncertainly without the familiar pull,
dropping quickly through to rest,
over long before we knew.
A barren field arises on the camera,
strewn perfectly—
randomly—
with a colorless array of stone,
large and small,
sweeping in a short inhuman arc
to the near horizon.

Then a tall and brutal mountain—
sharp, stark.
We welcome you, Gentlemen!
It's good to be home.

by PATRICK J. McDONALD, Bowdoin College, Me.

CONVOY

Railroad crossings spring
To attention their eyes flashing
At the sound of a whistle pulling
Itself into town.

All aboard jerk-slack-jerk
I sit down window-side
And watch the morning haze bounce
Over land toward Hoboken.

The train bends a turn
Streaking across dammed rain water
And ducks lift
Waving their handkerchief-wings
Over stone graves
Rising on a hillside.

And from this I sink back into memory;
Riding another train south
Stopping only to follow orders
Letting a freight
Bullet through sparkling on its parade
Of wheels
That vanish into a tunnel of night.

16

I see my-younger-self
Hands full with a card game
Laughing under a helmet of smoke
Making friends
By telling jokes that hide my basic fears
As we rattle closer to Jacksonville.

Mid-way we change cars
And bunk down in a row of Pullmans
Each room writing a letter
into snores.

Our train is met head-on
And air screams in a splitting of rails
As the flipped weight falls/dead
Scraping its side to earth
Its windows exploding over the landscape.

We climb from ceiling doors
And jump
Into gravel trenches
Standing our heads in line to be counted
Like cattle.

After hours
We are led down track
To board a procession of public coaches
Five hundred of us file
into the column-seats.

I leave my seat
And walk to the end of faces
Where I invade the privacy of a box-car
Marked mail
And sit among stacked men
Boxed for shipment
Each buried beneath a stenciled
Destination.

by GARY ARMSTRONG, Rockland Community College, N. Y.

17

Evening is just hanging in—
Its cool breath stirring the willows,
The crickets voicing their release
        from the sun's oppressive presence,
The greenness of my world melting
        into the irresistible shadow,
            Waiting shatters the crystal of my mind,
Imperceptibly blending
        Mind and matter
Image and reality.

by MAUREEN T. MALONEY, Georgian Court College, N. J.

WINTER GREEN

Right there, a pine-tree, bone—
White as a spine, reflects
December's noonday sun,
Responds to chilling
Hints of wind by blanching
The back of my neck with soggy
Snow.

And yet, some sooty pigeons,
Their plumpness bathed in melting light,
Quiver into the shallow blue, pry
Into a building-blunted
Sky, soar not once, but only
Sink as if on liquid
Wings.

That fine conviction of
Points sought to scratch the sun
Out with a storm of barbed wire,
A trilling stream of talons on
Which only cones could float
As ignited blossoms.

by DANIEL O'HARA, St. Joseph's College, Pa.

GYPSY DANCE

Bell-toed dancers glisten-armed whirl
In woods-cumbered circles
Of fire-rimmed worlds:
Falcon-eyed,
Shadow-shawled,
Silk-flashing girls
Knife rustle-clad steppings
In black-maelstromed swirls.

by HELEN C. MACK, Clark University, Mass.

I TOOK A WALK TODAY

I took a walk today to the harbor
down narrowing alleyways
where fish carts clattered,
smelling of cod, herring on ice—
odor of her Nantucket
that September when we watched
boats slogging in with the catch
under wheels of gulls,
and we hid among the dunes
and your back read the print
of grass and tiny shells.

I wonder how you are now.

This morning I saw
a face that looked like yours—
in a dress shop window
a mannequin stood undressed
for alterations. Then . . . then
her arms moved up to her face
and long fingers threw back
the fluted hair from her white neck . . .

19

I called your name—
and she looked at me.

A boat whistle shrills
at the wharf, and ships
with cranes like spiders
pack cargo in black holds.
I see a royal blue uniform
topped by a proud white cap,
standing in shadow.
An oblique slash of light
like a sabre drops the head.

I should protect you from the dark.

Floating on a barge
is a girl in silken chemise.
A man on the dock above her huffs,
"Where is your brassiere, donkey darling?"

I disappear like a searching echo.

by F. WILLIAM BINZER, Middlebury College, Vt.

XMAS '69

Imagine; me Merlin
Hooting like an owl
Turning my head all the way around
And living backwards.

But I have not passed the centuries
I am Grandfather who forgets in mid-sentence
And mumbles as my mind creeps forward
To youth and passion.

Christmas will be for me, the grandchild
Who is naive enough to believe
The lore of every street-bound Santa
And the brotherhood of Christmas shoppers.

I shall love the presents
But will I wonder why the pricetags
Are placed on joy and brotherhood
And doves are proper only now?

The sixties sizzled by
But still I lie an age away
Waiting on the nearest tree limb
Hooting Grandfather hoots.

by WARREN E. AVIS, JR., Brown University, R. I.

a norwegian viking taught me the dance of the wind
it was in springtime and we were both green between flowers
and green between flowers he loved me
tumbleweed and plum heather
together we walked on frozen northern waters
sinking into the earth's soft core
sailing upwards through each sea to the next
days later he sailed on alone

i thought for a long time that i would never want to sail again

a dutchman and i streamed past broken windmills
there were no tulips but many dunes
we beneath pine trees in sand sailing
the april morning held us closely
walking on white windblown castles
i ran ahead and he slid backwards
and i walked on alone

i still cannot walk in sand

the young david took my hand and taught me to roll wild
                              and naked down a hill again

it was not springtime
we did not mind

autumn sun slowly warms bodies to believe it is june
he turned me green again with his special yellow sun
i had not been longing for my dandelion ways
but he brought them back to me
winter was coming and with it the snow
i believed during our days that green and yellow could melt the
    snow
but it melted him
              and he me

inside of him are my secrets
he has them until i learn once again
                    to walk through sand and sea
and to climb a tree by myself

by **JODY BIKOFF, Carnegie Mellon University, Pa.**

YEARS, NOT THE SORROW

Four floors deep into the black moon,
In a compartment like a bomb,
An ageless shadow
Crossed her lips to a bulging child
And slipped under his bed.
There he looked, saw his sunken mother,
Cheeks dried to flesh, under bags bone-deep.
O, Mother,
Through nerves of glass you whispered,
Am I forgiven? Am I forgiven?,

While my father, hunched to tears by the job
He could lose, swore you bitterly into a grave
And searched you out,
Pouring his body of drunken rage
And grief over wall, table and chair,
Till his sight collapsed.
Later,
He would find my bed, wrap me in sobs,
Beg forgiveness. In the morning,
The gray morning, he would beg for yours,
In the morning that covered the ghosts
Of our days.

Forgive me.
Years after, I would drop my head
Over the bed's edge and look beneath;
There,
Beyond black,
I would see a hideous shape, be
Snatched, dragged under, without sound,
Beyond it, screaming, screaming
For my mother, my mother, my . . .

O, only the dawn, ashed and scarred, would wake me.
Years, not the sorrow would pass.
And now my mother, you are almost old,
And my father, who loves us,
I forgive you both.
But I cannot sleep.

by DENNIS GRUNES, State University of New York at Buffalo

CASUAL-TIES

"We have left the era of confrontation and entered the era of negotiation."

Wind-wheezing, the hardened web
mantles the sugared window ledge.
Stolen flour and molded tea
creak beneath the soured
milk floor. Behind the door
gold gleams like pebbled teeth.

NIXON ENTERTAINS DEFENSE DEPARTMENT
AT KEY BISCAYNE

As the litter whimpers
the hungry runt sighs
dividing stale crusts
palsied fruit and glued rice.
Six mice squeal in mincing harmony,
clamoring for crumbs.

JOINT CHIEFS OF STAFF WEEKEND AT
WESTERN WHITE HOUSE

Yet gold infests the gilt-lit room
in starving folds that plead of Pure.
The bleeding deepens every year, and now
they are not sure if the moth-proof
door will close.
Or open.

by **MARY-ANN HILDICK, Union College, N. J.**

U.

white haired
irene
    fiftynine years
    in the wind

serves tea
    with lemon

in the college cafe

        sea-eyed
        warm wrinkel'd
        russian breasted
        lady
        from the ukrain

sweet word
broken on her tongue
smile dangling
from her lips

      when she says
        tea?

i know nothing
      of irene
      beyond maid's apron
      and red creamed hands

      her desires
      her life is
      obscured to me

she might have
a husband somewheres

slumbering off
a drunk
on the floor of
a harlot

for all i know

by JOHN ANDERSON, Wagner College, N. Y.

FENESTA FRIENDSHIP

I met Fenesta Friendship yesterday.
She had been standing on a corner
waiting for a bus and I picked her up.
I remember she had a lovely rose
dress on. Its light material kept
blowing in the wind. From my mouth,
a long stemmed pipe made her laugh
as she waved her hand through the smoke
that curled around it. She moved close to me.
Her every word spoken in my ear
seemed to come from deep inside her,
I hoped from between her legs.
They did
and we kissed
on an empty forest road
after talking about the weather,
God,
an article in T.V. Guide
and
love.

by RONALD BAATZ, Fairleigh Dickinson University, N. J.

FUTIL FUTILITARIANISM

A fleck of time, a breath in space,
Reflection of life through a shallow face,
Pinnioned on the poignant pinnacle
Of motion moved by a motionless mover.

Tallyman tarries as the Draft cadence count
To their medium of measured plight,
Diurnal decadence of corporeity casts
Quick terminance to eternal tenure.

Lidless cadaver conscripted at conception,
Vain incendiary of inappeasable inanity
Forfends relentless the irrepealable reality.
Sole probity in passivism lies.

by JACK R. NINNIS, St. Joseph's College, Pa.

THE BRIDGE

The crickets that grow damp at night and glisten
In the grass on the near side of the ridge,
I've often wondered if they know I listen
While I'm playing solitary bridge.
By 11:30 the news is fully reported
And The Late Show to my dismay I saw last year,
Come Midnight my mind is acting vague, distorted,
That the chill of dark is urging me to sleep is clear.
One last smoke in bed, lamp on, sets me feeling drowsy.
I fill a glass with water, start the fan pulsating
To the evening's brew and ask of me "How's he
Going to shut his mind and stop it from relating?"
The room is dimly lit, the shade drawn, the curtains pulled across.
I turn to motorcycles, books I'd like to write, a girl
I miss and realize to stop it now would be a loss,
Then crack my toes and squirm about preparing for adventure.

With the light still on I down my glass of water
Waiting, pick up cards and deal to night's vibration.
The minister is West, someone else's daughter
North and East of course a marvelous sensation.
Cards all dealt my lonely crew begins to bid
Six spades or in a pinch four hearts will suffice.
Done, I amaze at how we communicated,
My partner and I in this endless time so nice.
Next East deals, then on and on around forever
And though it's fun I must confess my thoughts wander
Some and once a moustached man came and flipped the lever,
Drew me to that outside stuff of which I am much fonder.
Around four A.M. a strange bird or insect, living,
Yields an awful shriek and then one more, this nightless rover
From beyond the ridge, which is his way of giving
Me fair warning that the party's over.

by ANDREW R. FISHER, Amherst College, Mass.

A SEASON

Modulations of a strawberry summer mark the prelude—

Clouded premiere, etching that half smile on your face
To be evermore imprinted in the eventide of our
                                    inner-most thoughts.

Brambles so evasive
                    smothering the realm of our being.

Mauve of twilight
                burning for recognition.

Pompous caricatures intermingle. . . .

                    Dehydrated porcelain bodies
                                        kissed by the whims
                                        of yesterday.

28

Raw-boned delusions of summer's end—notched and scarred—

Motile feelings gush forward only to be
                              thwarted

Sophisticated songbird accents the beauty of your all

        while beats of 'the pain to come' remain soundless
                              covered up in cloths
                              of ecstasy.

Chapeau of Love escapes our clutches—flooding salty stains upon
                              our cheeks . . .

'Tis you oh haughty anticipated fever that we in our blindness
                              hurry to
        elect to be our omnipotent tolerant for
              the present
                      but
                      at long last
                              unrewarding.

Banish us if you must into the cool eyes of winter
                              for we can forget; but the
                      bloom of your resurrection will
                      begin the ascension of our oppressed
                      emotions.

Sandpaper breezes—we know what you tell us—but our ears do
                              not hear; we
                      are mute in your presence

revolving existence of Now
                      your spokes are turning slowly . . .
                              Is this the
                              end?

by KATHY REID, Paterson State College, N. J.

CANNERY ROOF

Up the hill and five feet down
On the cool slick tiles
Bordered by broken mortar
Hot bodies twine and brush the sand
Gathered in the roofing cracks
And crush the growing aster plants
Into pungent slippery pulp

Down five yards from the nearest tomb
Warm hands smooth hands
Touch shoulders slicked with sweat
And scrape the concrete wall that half surrounds
Two people up from the cannery roof
And down from the tombsone hill
Walk silent neither looking
And only touching hands

by VICTORIA A. FARR, Mansfield State College, Pa.

SEA OF TRANQUILITY

And to this barren sea of dust once chaste
    An alien called Man
        Has come to pay his doleful homage
            To a star

Being welcomed (long awaited) as a corpse
    Accepts its first late mourners
        Who lean close and almost touching
            Lifeless nothing

Reraise their heads
    Close a tear upon the eye
        And peer beyond the grayness
            Burying corpses
To see stars.

by L. R. ALBERT, Pennsylvania State University

30

CODY, WYO.

We crawl beyond roadsigns as sun
and clouds separate like a cracking egg.

We are spinning or the world is spinning.
We may not be moving at all.

Not passing slat houses and street markers
and whipping trees. We drive

and drive until we are insensible
with fatigue and coffee and no one knows

where we are from
or where we are going.

We want to stop, roll down
the windows, and shout to the man

who stands by the highway
that we are different,

that we are making our way where
we have not been before. But we do not.

Slovenly, like pigs eating dried white corn
we count miles and all that

is new in us vanishes except when
the sky opens, thunders, and our tires bloat

and ride smoothly on glass, and the pupils
of our eyes dilate in the clean bright light.

by **MARIANNE JOHNSON, Syracuse University, N. Y.**

PARABLE

Aunt Sally loved that boy.
She would have sold her soul for him.
If anything ever happens to him, she swore,
I'll die.

But of course she didn't.
She lived a million years and
Her mind stayed razor sharp and clear
So she could not forget.

And all the years she raged.
Oh, how she raged!

Where is your mercy, Lord, she cried,
You who dare call yourself Lord,
Where is your mercy?

Her voice rang out unbridled to the heavens,
Past the moon and the stars and even, finally,
To Him. And He, caressing the child with love,
Listened, and was puzzled.

Aunt Sally loved that boy.
She would have sold her soul for him.
Perhaps she did.

by MARIE WOOD, Paterson State College, N. J.

HOROSCOPE

Into the fast-filling wastebasket of my life
I dropped you . . .
You were, like me, a Taurus
Destined under the same star
To lock horns in mortal-immortal combat.

We even fought over the proper grammatical plural
    for our sign.
All-American, you argued for "two Tauruses."
The Latin scholar in me rebounded with "a pair of Tauri."
"What's all the fuss about?" you asked.
"We're just a couple of bulls."
Couple of coupling, animal husbandry,
"What's the name for a lady bull? A bullet?"
"Bully for you. I'm a cow."
The evening spoiled by semantic misunderstanding,
We retreated to opposite sides of our domestic pasture:
You, behind a Hemingway-novel wall,
And I, into a daydream
Of Libra, with Scorpio rising.

by ELIZABETH LOWE, Paterson State College, N. J.

My lady wore a ruby
Pigeon's blood
Men called it
Though men's blood
Made it
So my lady wore it

Pigeons—bastard cousin
Of the dove
Perhaps the dove's blood
Made it
So my lady wore it

by C. R. WILLIAMS, Wilkes College, Pa.

PIONEER WOMEN

Wagon wheelexistence of life
Vying for a peaceful coexistence
With Madam Nature.
Sending out husbands
Hoping they will return
Bulletless and arrowless.
Finding new diseases
To test physical strength.
Bearing children into the world
Knowing not whether bearer
Or borne will survive.
Counting as luxuries
Clear star nights
Rain-dripped violets
Children's laughter.
Children to carry on.
Men to build dreams
Women to build nations.

by PAMELA SIMONES, Vassar College, N. Y.

VISION

Last night my mind ran along the paths of my eyes
to the blinking eyes of the highway through the trees.
Sweeping pattern of lights, darks, and lives
Filling the night void, calling to me from the blackened mouth
of the road. A mirthful voice from a throat of gravel,
a shivering laugh from shoulders of stone.

Running to where my eyes had walked, I listened
for the secret voice that had beckoned me so many times.
I smiled and waited on my busy friend, only to hear
the ugly scream of empty tires.

With lowered eyes, and shapeless thoughts
I left.
And
heard her whisper
Farewell

by STEVEN RAIKEN, State University of N. Y. at Buffalo

MOLOCH'S LAST STILLBIRTH

We are in danger of becoming part of the brick
    of the building;
what divides us is that we are softer
    and have reflecting eyes.

Moloch awaits with his teeth bared
    and his thousand blind eyes flashing;
    his breath is carbon monoxide,
    his saliva is scum from unclean lakes,
    his voice is a flock of frustrated geese
    sounding animal jealousy.
He consumes with a sweep of his hollow
and bigoted mouth—he searches out people
    with his calloused, blunt tongue
    and there is no sympathy
    to those sensitive to people.
His presence is announced loudly over the microphone
    and we pretend to pray at meals
    when our souls are really
    our stomachs.
Moloch howls and some run to help
    the humanicide (today a new type of death);
    they childishly grasp the microphone for him
    and their bite stings like
    a limp mosquitoe—and we try not to hate.

35

Where were you Paul Goodman when you warned us
            of people becoming
            extensions of the institutions
            rather than vice versa—somewhere
            within the shadow of a sick skyscraper
            no doubt.
Moloch is pretentious and he is in love with
            his voice.
He has pitched camp nearby—he is an ugly monster
            and we try harder to love.
Moloch's helpers cry "we understand"
            and they guide us—we are tin soldiers:
            some of us flinging
            ourselves into the fire,
            others dying at the base of trees,
            some of us reaching cloudy boughs
            to spy on Moloch;
            too many waiting for Moloch
            to breathe fire
            and we plan against Moloch.
Moloch has tortured the countryside
            with blind buildings breathing fire;
            the living day he has turned into
            a speeding clock ticking away people.
            He has blasphemed mankind—hindering
            love with false modesty
            and the fear to love—
            our tears are shed for friends (let us sacrifice) .
Moloch is not a conquering hero—
            he is a treacherous bastard with
            no sons or lovers and no real love
            except his hatred.
            He has made enemies with Sons and Lovers and upset
            early spring playmates spotting green hills.

            We have passed Delphi to a field of
            delicate dandelions
            warm against the wind and there are friends
            of green growing
            on our side.

With our love we have planned
a silent death for Moloch—
revolution's heartbeat has moved
the surface of love.
There is a silver, creeping stream,
less violent than Moloch's blood,
beyond the fever of the field
and Moloch will drown—shalom Moloch.

by GABRIEL R. RICCI, St. Joseph's College, Pa.

SIGHT AND INSIGHT

Frost-fallen are the leaves
    that turn bare branches
    into traceries of lace
        against the sky
    and not till then
        did I
    the shape of trees
        more fully know.
Dismantled of green contours
    all the gnarled and bent
        groan greyly
    for their final cloak
        of fringe-flaked snow.

How like the heart
    by life's short spring and summer
        greenly gowned!

37

All scarcely known
    till scarlet autumn ends
with winter's leaflessness,
    and then we stand
        stripped strangely in sad shapes
    life-long our own;
in such unrealized reality
    the eyes that saw
        but saw not say,
"I never knew this was the way
    her heart would look."

by RUTHE T. SPINNANGER, Paterson State College, N. J.

ACADEMIA

Aqaba, Da Nang
How ugly, how real.
Escape to an Island
Called Hemingway, the Land
of Yeats.
More respectable and allowable than
Oz.
(But only slightly more so.)
In case of atomic attack
The safest place to be
is in
The Renaissance.

by JAMES J. MARTINE, Pennsylvania State University

JUNE

Red roses basking in the sun.
Green leaves leaning over fences.
Hot pavement making bare feet dance.
Black tar melting in highway cracks.
Thirsty grass yearning for water.
Brown birds babbling to each other.
White ice cream trucks ringing bells
To lure laughing children from their play.
Young couples strolling hand in hand
On warm, white sand.

by CONNIE RAE BEAVEN, Columbia Union College, Md.

Why am I fixated by reality's legions by the Arabs and the cold
    women
Of the tribe Lawrence of Arabia has a mask on his face he is
    an Arab

A Bedouin a thief in the night a castrato a recluse a waster
Of women and I am evil itself personified by my desires and
    seen in my wants

What are my wants? You, baby, I want you my Arab lady I
    want your black skin back
Up against me I want your body back

Up against me I want to climb on top of you
And drive my anger through your heart and give you death and
    love together on one knife of need and cut your body
    so you recover only the pieces only the pieces and
    never the whole thing again.

by NORMAN STOCK, Hunter College, N. Y.

39

When old Jack Arthur
mentioned Henry was dead
and, seeing my face, said,
"Oh, I'm sorry.
I thought you knew:
that dog was runnin' deer right through
the Game Lands. He was shot."
Well, I told him
it didn't matter anyhow,
that dog was good-for-nothing.
Couldn't call him a cow-
dog, that's for sure.
He was just an old hound
that Mary liked. Hung around
the barn when I was milking.
Good-for-nothin'—I told him that.

From the time he was a pup
he was nothing but trouble.
Got caught in a fox trap
and I had to stumble
my way all through the swamp one night
trying to find him yipping.
He lost three toes.
God knows
Why I didn't shoot him then.
He used to raise one hell
of a noise when I'd
come home. Turn inside
out with his damned wagging.

Sometimes at night
after Mary died,
he'd climb on my bed and hide
near my feet, fool dog.
And not a brain in his head
for rabbit-running.

He'd get off the track
and come bounding back
wiggling—'specting praise.
Mary didn't raise
him right with her talkin' and feedin': Hand-
picked every scrap. Told him things
no dog could understand.

He crawled 'neath the house
the day she died.
Fool dog, never was very bright.
Running deer, you said?
Well, he's better off dead.

by JOAN ZELKOWITZ, Wesleyan University, Conn.

I AM THE GRASS

The fragrant lies of springtime
    call young lovers into the meadows.
I am the grass.
I see passing lovers come and go.
They lie among my leaves.
Their bodies crush me;
    my juice runs dying green and sere
    and stains their limbs with my departing life.
    Lying there they unite and become one with me
    while the day flows by to afternoon, then evening . . .
And after they have gone, the night reminds me of them,
    for they covered me from the day
    with searing breath and starry words
    while with lightly closed eyes they experienced
    the seasonal truth.

41

I am the grass.
I see lovers come and go,
     taking a part of me with them when they leave.
I do not mind.
They will return to me again someday.

by JOHN WHITE, Yale University, Conn.

THE WOLF

Autumn, indefatigable wolf

Marie, Marie, of creole blood

After an evening with Austen,
he took you home in the train
to his mother's house in the
suburbs, and furthermore,
left you there until it was
discovered you had creole blood

Autumn, Autumn
indefatigable wolf

swallowing leaves, while Marie
wears her straw hat back to the city.

by GAYL JONES, Connecticut College

GENESIS SYNTHESIS

Slithering out onto
    primeval shore
mud snail .
      pondered creation
sniffed and smelled
    breeze
        sand
           surf
wiggled antennae
         for kind response
the breeze said cold
    the sand cooed mushy
      the surf cried harsh
mud snail weeped
    "To Hell with it all"
and slithered back to sea.

by WILL COLLETTE, Rhode Island Junior College

DIRECTIONS

Through an arch
the garden spreads
where gods once stood
now statues with painted lips
silently motion in stone

and whisper to
the gathered faithful
"Consider all this merely a question raised."

at the gate
Our Lady of Illusion
smiles on all
three quarter believers
and asks no questions.

by SONIA HAMMAM, State University of New York at Potsdam

43

I have drunk of three chalices
the first a pure silver vessel,
    beat smooth metal
    containing a sweet wine
    bringing an ecstasy

the second a handcrafted one
    decked out
    with exotic detail
    the earthy brew flowing o'er
    o'er in profusion

the third goblet I found
in an antique store
    full of old legend
    and curiously wrought
I brought it home and drank its brew:
    gall
and I knew that I had tasted
of the stuff of life.

by CHRISTINE WOLFE, Carlow College, Pa.

HOW DULL IT IS TO MAKE AN END

Services ended at the mission church
with only still pews in the empty nave;
While putting up gowns and altar clothes
I questioned my profits as preacher.
John Eliot dealt to this Indian race
the laws and commands of Powerful Goodness,
and also taught of the tempter's ways.
I sermoned this hoard with pious heart . . .
though some had slept.
'By the devil tempted forty-days
and went without the slightest food;
Beware his attack on your weak flesh!'

Through my teachings I made a name,
and though some slept, they knew me.
John Eliot knew and shared his faith,
for them to repel their evil ways.
They now knew of the tempter's fate,
his battle with Goodness and Adam's fall.
They gave me honor for what they knew
of the Powerful Goodness and my useful tool.
They had taken much but I knew much more.
John Eliot taught the word of Goodness;
and also taught of the tempter's ways.
How dull it is to make an end,
when asked the sleepy savage:
"Why God not kill the Devil?"
and I could not answer.

by **MICHAEL CICHOWSKI, Seton Hall University, N. J.**

TOWARD A MYTHOLOGY OF PEARS

Sometimes
it's like a private joke.
Your period's late and you'll be talking
                              about babies
and the years will tumble by like orchards
of jackrabbits. (I'll smile to myself.)
I won't tell you the punchline.
There's too little time
for sadness.
It's like eating pears by oneself.

by **LEONARD B. TERR, Brown University, R. I.**

in unconscious winter
i have come to thaw
by red and white woolen scarves
and flower-painted mugs of cocoa
in closed-windowed rooms
where peace comes quiely.

like still-warm chocolate
and feathered flakes of snow
melting
i sing whispered songs of gratitude.

by SISTER MARIA CARDINAL, College of St. Rose, N. Y.

THE FIRST DEAD

their sticks of war cross
and bind us together once.
the quick robbers remember
their death, not the dying.
my collapse, jerked by shot,
was not a dance for them;
my rattle, silent now,
was not a song nor hymn;
my rain punctured body
will not compost their rebirth
now that we are one.

by LYNN AULICK, Bryn Mawr College, Pa.

SUMMER LOVE

"Love is the veil between lover and lover"
                                KAHLIL GIBRAN

The world shone bright every morning.
Nimbus was turned to Nymph
As the thousand Cupids raced
Frantically about happy Heaven's imagination
World.

Green pillows and daisied sheets
Spread beneath us on endless
Wedding day's witching-hours.
No tidalwave of trials
Could wash the joy from our hearts.

But the weather changed in early Autumn.
And the cold winds disturbed
Not only our meadow.

The knowing hand, that would close
Telepathically over mine, ceased.
And though you smiled, our eyes
would seldom meet.
The once caressing, tiny laugh
Now curdled in your throat, and
My heart choked on every word
From your cautious lips.
The mason was busily at work
In everything you did then.
The wall took shape with bricks
Of ridicule and suspicion—
Strengthened with mortar from the
Sand of change that drifted between us
During our Summer of love.

I would give a pirate's treasure
To know what took place
In that dune-shifting desert
You call your mind.

by JOSEPH MEREDITH, La Salle College, Pa.

WHAT GREEK DANCE ANSWERS YOUR GREEN UNSATISFIED SEEDS O PERILOUS PRIEST?

Originals of sin and sanity
sing in a land of lions & plums.
Do not say the bleak obliquities of speech
have made of savage air an airless thing
or scraped feathers from your life among ferns.
Because death your hands beyond knowing sweetly know
how trees (like crazy ladies) and all the crackling dragons
consort like fleas and challenge you to
feast, in a brave & sacred place to peer
at mysteries of fish with invisible fins;
not to touch or finish but—behold—

your eyes are lions which begin.

by PAMELA ALEXANDER, Bates College, Me.

SCHOOL'S OUT

They are gone
The professors drove away
Lesson plans are of no concern
The pool sharks took their sticks
Their "reps" are intact even in defeat
The demonstrators leave their placards

48

Issues are of no concern
The Sisters and Brothers split
They took their bad rap to the street
The scholarly students finally pause
Grades of "A" are of no concern
The friends are all gone
In truth, I know that all of them
Made school exactly what it was
And shall always be; for,
My mind's grey walls covet
Each cherished memory.

by GEORGE STEVENS, Delaware State College

I DIDN'T KNOW

Sitting there I didn't know
that she was a grandmother
or that she was Jewish.
I didn't know she had moved
to New York from Massachusettes
in the winter of 1947.
I couldn't tell her oldest
son was a neurosurgeon in Texas
and her daughter married a Gentile.
I didn't know her husband
had been a lieutenant on the
New York City police force
for twenty years.
I couldn't tell that she had
enjoyed doing needlepoint and
once made a sampler for her grandson
saying GOD IS LOVE or that
her brother had died at
thirty seven years from a monkey
bite he got at the laboratory
where he had been employed.

I didn't know she had lost a
pair of twins at birth right
in her own house on Tyng Street.
Sitting there on the body length
concrete grave stone all I knew
was that Ethel Davis was
born on March 7, 1873, and
had died on November 1, 1958.

by MARILYN J. WHITEHEAD,
Rockland Community College, N. Y.

WILLIAM CARLOS WILLIAMS AND THE PLUM

(For Suzy—after a Conversation about Pappas)

Suzy spoke of her Grandfather,
    "Pappas"
poet, philosopher
        humble man
    who wrote all the time
(who had a new way of facing things)

One night he stared
at the plum sitting lonely
    in the refrigerator
    and he wrote a poem to
        the plum
    and in the morning, awoke
        and in a frenzy
        ate his evidence
    but, the poem
        remains today
            as proof.

by ANITA L. HOLZBERG, Paterson State College, N. J.

AS THE CURTAIN FALLS

From the first slap upon my buttocks,
    I started toward death.

A series of stages:

        Infancy.
        Childhood.
        Adolescence.

And then, when the maturation process has
    been completed,
I am returned to soil and, in essence, to
    the dust whence I came.

Throughout these stages we are conscious of
    the Final Act.
And the Final Act is conscious of us.

Then the strings are played and the puppets
    move back and forth across these earthen
    planks.

Bravo,
Bravo.
                  But no encore.

by **WILLIAM BLANCHARD, Fairleigh Dickinson University, N. J.**

FOR BABY JENNY

    be gentle the winds
    that on your consciousness
    dance
    the beat of the dying
    that makes your strength
    grow limper

rampant you run
pressed to my hand
ethereal
over pillowy marigold
folds catching feathery
petals
in your feet

among the trees
billowing golden sandals
the fleeting breeze
dabbles to rest
the barefooted light

in them you bower
the cradle limped
by my hand
rocking the sway
of airy sleep

kissed
by the light
receding of radiance
you sink into slumber
lulled by the murmurs
of leafy whispers

by GEORGE WEN, Dartmouth College, N. H.

AHAB
OR, GOING TO THE SEA

(M.L.K.—d. April 4, 1968)

*"Leviathan maketh a path to shine after him;
One would think the deep to be hoary."*

JOB

1.   GOING TO THE SEA

Call him Ahab,
in the habit of going to the sea.
        Going to the sea
when the land became too much,
being too little.
        Going to the sea,
casting himself into its murderous,
life-giving swells.
Casting himself out from the soothing,
strangling strands of the shore.
        Going to the sea
as a sailor.
As a sailor, as a part of the grand
program of Providence.
        A part of the grand
program, a footnote reading:
"Whaling voyage by one Ahab."

2.   THE WHITENESS OF THE WHALE

One Ahab
        going to the sea,
being lured by an odor in the air.
        Going to the sea,
being lured by the whiteness of the whale.

the whiteness of the whale
the whiteness
the pure
untouched
snowy
sunless
piercing
terror of
the whiteness of the whale.
Going to the sea,
being lured to the chase.

3. THE CHASE

The chase,
the long, luring chase.
So long, it seemed a lifetime.
So long, so many lifetimes.
So many sightings,
so many harpoons,
so many shattered boats,
so long.

And then
from the slate sea shot
the white whale.
Again! Again! Again!
The big ship was pounded, splintered,
pounded, panicked.
Again! Again! Again!
Incredibly.

And then
the quarter-deck was empty.

The sea,
beaten white hot, subsided.

The monster
fish resumed its narrow path.

But, even now,
harpoon line wound roun its neck,
the heaving corpse of Ahab rolls
across the mad, red eye
of the great, white whale.

by M. CHARLES McANULLA, St. Johns University, N. Y.

INCIDENT

It was exactly
Nine thirty-one—
I know;
Coffee break
Was only just done,
When the cement bucket's
Four-story flight
Was suddenly stopped dead
By the muscley hod-carrier's
Kinky brown head.
"My God!"
Cried the Foreman
And hurried to
Investigate.
(Of course when he got there
It was much too late)
Quite a mess it was
All over the mud;
The Puerto Ricans wouldn't touch it
For fear of the blood.
So they called up the Super,
Said, "Come right on,
There's been an accident,
No work's getting done."

55

And we all stood and looked
    at the bloody smashed head
    at the brains on the walk
    at the sight of the dead
    at the allseeing eyes
And silence buzzed like flies.
Until the dozer-driver, McDooley,
An incorrigible sort,
Covered up the damn thing,
And we went back to work.

by JAMES M. TABOR, University of Vermont

TO PROFESSOR CALDWELL

That He May Survive

He sat enthroned today,
aloof among his books,
literally alone,
though I had come to call—
I, quick with confidence,
an unread, unshaped youth
who judged him set in stone.

"If you can sing," he spoke
at last, in sharp refrains
of hope, to crack meaning's
mask, "then remember me."
And suddenly I could see
quite through him, through his books,
why he so summoned me.

by KENNETH JOHN ATCHITY, Yale University, Conn.

PENSEE

I speak out;
The frost clings
and people go on their way.
Each isolated in his own.
Let the moment of 11 p.m.
on seventy-second Street and
Broadway be frozen and only
the snow come
as a glass winter scene
paper weight
upside down.
Alone I stand as I wait
for the crosstown bus,
a drunk passes,
respectable,
I get on the wrong bus.

by NANCY JANE KEATS, New York University, N. Y.

MOONRISE

(To Those Killed in the War)

Awakened
On a muggy midsummer's night,
Awakened
By the on-rush of white light—
Light bright in a world of black!

There it called-out painfully:
The moon, man-trod now, spoke
As it reached-out through the oak
That extended a hand mournfully—

It called me from black-rose-dreams,
Called for praise, called for prayers—
   The moon held-hands, white beams
Mirrored in mortal eyes: it cried on deaf ears.

Awakened
On a muggy midsummer's night,
Awakened
By the on-rush of white light—
Light bright in a world of black!

Moon and Man touched:
   But the Moon is not comforted by it!
Moon and Sea embrace:
   And life flows-out for roses that sit
Upon the cold tombs of soldiers gone back—

Gone back, but not to war;
Gone back to be awakened
By a midsummer's moonrise
Upon that other shore—
Gone back to be awakened
By a midsummer's moonrise . . .

by **BR. RICHARD MATERA, FSC,**
Catholic University of America, Washington, D.C.

THE WATERFALL

I jumped over the waterfall
Out of Paradise,
Out of the silent water
Beneath the pallid ice,
Over the edge in a storm of foam
And into a green glass tower,
Into the midday twilight
Under the foam-flake shower;

Over my body the fragments fell,
Pounding me into the stream.
I am caught in the turbulent movement
Of river-mud-maiden's dream.

by KATHERINE W. RYLAARSDAM, Smith College, Mass.

Miranda of the Misty Mount searches
                    (with drowning eyes)
for a lover she has never known.
Her love-winged feet carry her swiftly
through the labyrinth of the populace
while she searches numberless eyes
for a quality she has never known.
And of a sudden she stops her quest,
  (Her weary heart desires rest)
She cries, she thinks she's done her best.
and then . . .
A throbbing in her chest she feels
as her restless eyes meet his—
the Lover she has never known
(and his name is Truth)

by WILLIAM SULLIVAN, Fordham University, N. Y.

HOW TO BE A CRITIC WITHOUT REALLY TRYING; OR, GRADUATE SCHOOL MADE SIMPLE

For your teachers, quick, to snow'em
Call some random words a poem.
Next this poem 'gin to judge
Solely on its language.

Then, devise a way to mention
That you're sure its major tension
Clearly shows a para-chronic
Use of the technique ironic.
Under pain of lasting schism
Always praise its varied rhythm;
And bluntly hint it's widely known
The poem well controls its tone.
And (lest the poem seem mechanic)
Demonstrate its form's organic.
Lastly, prove thou this by any logic twirled:
That the po'm creates a world
Whose articulate concision
Makes't a vital verbal vision.
Thus, if all is done as I have said,
Pass you must as Man Learned.
And none but fools would ever doubt
That from these terms thoughts ne'er peeped out.

by PETER HAGGERTY, Rutgers University, N. J.

The sun seeps in over rolled sleeves
shaping the cornered pool of night
hunchbacked beside me.

Curled elm leaves hang over the
ground like breathless dust;

and the sleek hum of dungflies
melts into sun-soaked morning . . .

Last cold night the towering spruce
spears got lost in the stars like mist,

and everywhere I walked was
the center of the earth.

by BRUCE LIPPINCOTT, Eastern Connecticut State College

SHOPPING IN SEOUL

Chained to strings from an internal composition
of mixed thrusts; December in a violin wind of
soft snarls and faint sobs, I twitched my murky
eyes into the cutting kisses of morning in an
alleyway of seasoned clay.

Hu Am Dong, the market strip of you and I in
another place, another time. The narrow stretch
of cotton candy beards and horseshoe backs; the
old, retracing time on warted canes in mud and
urine. Polo shirts pressed against a steamed
window; the young, pursuing Jesus in a bakery
shop of jellied joints and dusty flesh. Milky
eyes perched on slimy crates; the halfwit saints,
enduring the moldy page of slippery words and
soggy crumbs of contradiction.

My sandy mind churned to bows and frigid steps
from banana shoes. The world displayed by cold
smiles and sunken bones. Apples, pears, lemons,
fruitcakes, cookies, tangerines, oranges, gum,
chestnuts. Chickens and roosters. Brooms and
shovels. Pots and pans. Hot peppers, garlic,
green onions, turnips, potatoes, ginger, squid,
cabbage; kimchi jars and life till spring. Tin
homes and cardboard doors. Straw baskets for
laundry heads and paper walls to hush the slosh
of prized retreats.

Another place, another time. Coney Island after
the crowds had gone. Music in savage notes from
loose wires, taut ropes and stiff canvas flapping
to the void. You and I, at home with the flat
tune of shuffles and forgotten papers, squirmed
to the uncut pebbles running the gaunt cheeks of
gritty thoughts and tender recognitions in brittle
seesaw rides and multiple masks on the other side
of the same clay.

by **MICHAEL HOOD**, Niagara University, N. Y.

I sit—my feet being chilled
Ever so lightly
The music chiming in the back—
Everything coming together
To Form
Serenity
Nothing artificial
Yes, this is a summer afternoon
This is peace and solitude
And seemingly a time for
Nothing—
No great desires
No sorrow—nothing
not even the good peaceful feeling
Because it is there and into it
am I so that I need not feel
it. It just is—And somewhere
Deep inside—like a small pebble
tucked away amongst the boulders
in My mind The reality—the knowing
rests quietly
One gets desires when one fears time is short
And I feel no such emotion—
Forever—I shan't go home—I shall journey
for it is somewhat you know—I shall journey
to another city
This is infinitely better than summer (camp) days off
Why—it's simple
The day off there is a mere change of scenery People are still
    with us
Here it is a time for yourself. But not so much self as just
a good feeling—One feels so inspired—Trying to

by **RICHARD PETERS**, Union College, N. Y.

GOING HOME FOR HALLOWEEN
(for Matthew)

We bickered away the morning until
The man loaded the biggest one
Into Jimmy's Pontiac. A gigantic one,
The color of a small boy's heart,
With vines still curling around it
Like mustaches.

You were disguised when we got back,
Delighted with your game of fooling,
And you laughed and scampered, wren-like,
Around the newspapers, while
I knelt the whole afternoon
Trying to make the pumpkin smile for you.

But weekends never last
More than two days, two hours, the time
It takes to scrape a pumpkin clean.
How many times have I hugged you good-bye,
Wondering if you'd still remember
Me when I returned?

I gather myself together:
Weekends have their place and this one
Is empty now. You can see
Me from your window and I wave,
Then pick up the suitcase, the rotting shell
And start back.

by SHEILA AMTZIS, State University of N. Y. at Cortland

And you pull this ugly
Stiff and frigid "thing"
From you,
Bashing its skull bloody
To balm the sore
Caused by its lack.
The dream clumps to the *floor*,
Twisted, rigid, motionless.

Its life is gone forever,
Like an Infant bird
Fallen from a hopeful nest
To the sidewalk,
Or a kitten
Still-born.

On a lightless
Empty night
A worm-carrying bird,
A wearied mother cat,
And a dreamer
Plod in night procession,
Taking their unrealized future
To a dark, tomblike corner.

by JIM KOCH, State University of N. Y. at Oswego

HOPE

Dark is silent against the foaming sea.
Dusk deepens and
I stand alone in the rain.
Spirits fall
As gray hope gathers all
Isolation in tears of pain.

Blue depths radiate green glows
As the world grows
To obscure innocence.
Helpless
I heed the presence of billowy white.

by SISTER WILLIAM MARIE GRACON, C.R.
The College of St. Rose, N. Y.

THE END
(Based on a woodcut by Albrecht Durer)

> *"God is teaching us to live, as if he didn't exist."*
> DIETRICH BONHOEFFER

God, in his infinite mercy,
I pray to see.
Christ, the Judge,
sitting on swords,
telling someone
to go to Hell.
& I, in repose,
in a mahogany box,
am buried with obsessions
& preoccupations.
(Children believe in schooldays,
God, and playing in the afternoons.)
In the end,
we forgot to believe in children.
I saw the lily, in Christ's ear.
He was telling someone
to go to Hell,
(quite unmercifully).

by CARL ROSENSTOCK, Union College, N. Y.

RAINY DAY SCENE

As if the sky destroyed itself and cluttered the ground;
as if the carrousel tree spiraled out of its roots
and skipped over that ocean;
as if the bell clanged fists
that pounded waves out of the water;
as if confetti spewed out of buildings
into this circus ring . . .
but rain drowns in the earth,
and roots hold the tree back from the brass ring,
and the bell fades in the smothering fist of the air;
but confetti paves the circus ring,
and layer by layer marries each performance.

by STEPHEN McKINNEY, University of Maine

DEAD

The little worm squirms and drowns
on a cruel rain-drenched concrete sea;

the insignificant snail crawls on,
determined to cross its stretch of ashes,
expiring punctually in the cool evening;

the tiny lightning-bug blinks its hopeful little lamp
in brief torrid August twilights,
going cold and out with the first fall chill;

the last brave fly flounders desperately
on an October windowsill,
finally succumbing to the unconcerned pane;

the young god lies among the carrion
and the stench rises.

by DONALD W. MILLER, Millersville State College, Pa.

THE WAFER AND THE POPE

Silken ropes, said the hawk
bind the willing and the old
and dove
with a doubting croak
to pluck my wordless eyes
my eyes and sightless nights
from aisles of kneeling lies.

And now, the blind
leads them all, he cried
and bowed
to me and
called me God.

by **THOMAS FRIEDMANN, Brooklyn College**

THE GOLDEN BOY REFLECTS

We were between the thin poetry volumes of houses,
Demanding the streets be sidewalks
When the Golden Boy called us over
To his Village doorstep;
He, friend of Odets, you know,

(The newspaper clippings testify);
G.B.'s life unfolds on stage,
The play's bones his bones;
He, friend of Edna St. Vincent Millay:
They stood together in a photograph for a moment;

The Golden Boy drew admiration from a stranger's concentration
Like a syringe sucking at a bottle of adrenaline,
Feeling sudden a thin self-esteem,
Like a sun-shower on a scorching summer day;

Thumbing through the yellowed stories
His eyes side-spoke past us
Out across the annual rings of sounds and buildings,
Diaphanous memories cling to brick crevices,
The textures of a filmy lifetime;
His face no longer composed for us,
We walked away, while he sat by his doorstep
With a billfold full of ashes—honey pooled deep in his lap—
Backstepping.

by CURTIS SLEPIAN, Harpur College, N. Y.

GRANDMOTHER

She sits
stiffly in the asylum
of the afflicted,
        her eyes

        sunken,
her skin, powder
sifted with dust,
        And milkless

        breasts.
Her bones
have fallen out.
        Frozen

        moments
hang in jars
around her neck,
        Her peace is

        our disease;
our parent,
our terror.
        We watch

the nimbus
radiate its death
around her head,
wait for

a sign.
We bring flowers
to turn away
her eyes.

by FRANCINE M. WEBER, Barnard College, N. Y.

LIGHT GAMES ON TELEGRAPH HILL

Lightly on yew tops
tiptoe silk slippers,
empty heels grazing
leaves as dust wakened by windy mops and
toes leaping over spots from cars climbing
above the city,
where buildings swirl light,
night neons of electric air,
while higher buildings
sleep between sheets of
low fog. Fireflies, like lost ships,
carry lanterns shining dots upon
waves dark and green.
Light plays lightly on loose air
as pink slippers leap leaves
soon to sprout puppet legs
bodiless in the breeze.
Pajama flaps cover pink slippers;
high yews push for sun.

by PAUL WEINBERG, Brown University, R. I.

CHORES

Frost covered the ground
As though it owned each acre.
Possessing each blade
As it defied the sun's glare.

An old compost pile
Silhouetted in the mist,
A symbol of chores,
Awaited the Baron frost.

by SUSAN KAY CAMPBELL, Keene State College, N. H.

"CURSE"

I remember the spring in Warsaw
With the faces of penitence
All my parent's friends carried.
There was a bush of evergreen
On Crakow Street near the market
That was placed, a memorial
To my parents and brothers.
They were drawn and quartered
To celebrate the Easter
Of nineteen forty-three.
They say the bush is a tribute
To such brave martyrs . . .
But I thought only Christians
Could be declared martyrs
And be made fodder for bushes
That bring tears to men's eyes.

by RONALD MARTIN SALZER, City College, N. Y.

WAVES

Standing by the water's edge,
I watch the moving hills,
with snow capped peaks,
glistening,
then disappearing.
Only to pop up again on some other swell.
As if running to greet my feet,
bare and carefree.
Thundering closer and closer,
I watch the wave roll in.
As if she were running,
to tell me of some exciting experience from the depths.
So innocent,
yet so powerful.
I watch her grow.
Changing form,
but never soul.
She reaches to touch my mind.
I want to take her home.
What fantasy.
She crashes at my feet,
as if begging me to listen to her pleas,
for peace,
for love,
for friendship.
Reaching out,
I run to catch her.
She slips away with the quickness of a cat.
Getting closer,
I wade deeper into her mind.
Sand swirling underfoot,
she tries to take me with her.
Wet with fear,
I run back to the dryness of a dune,
so I can watch the waves come in,
without becoming involved.

by JOHN GAGLIARDI, Morris Harvey College, W. Va.

71

VISITING HOME: ON MY FATHER
AWAKENING

She clicked the light and shook him from his dream.
He woke up small in the scarred oak bed,
Eyes red with fighting the insistant hunger
That was the only danger in 1933
In Chippewa County; he woke up curled up,
Dream-caught, confused, broke open his small knot,
Bunched like a shot squirrel, and stretched stiffly.
"I know he's here, I know," he said, coming slowly
From those old forests, "I'm awake." But his eyes
Wouldn't come to today. The wide silence
Of the hunt held him, and he looked past us,
Intent, still searching trees for nests, still searching
Through those devouring leaves for that small meal,
That dark meat for the many who must feed
On the illegal rabbit, the forbidden squirrel,
For it is summer, and all game is out of season,
As if hunger had a season but to eat.
But no. I cannot blind his eye-dark dream
With the electric bulb of 1966.
Turn out the light. I turned out the light.
I, who have never been bound to single-shot
And lead-shock for the daily sake of family,
Who killed perhaps ten bottles, and once, one slow squirrel,
Cannot forbid him gun, trees, squirrel, hunger again,
Cannot deny him his man-making pain.

by **WILLIAM HEDRINGTON, New College, Fla.**

FUGUE: DOCTOR FAUSTUS

Now strident, now racing, delicate
and sudden. Interchange of pursuer
and pursued. Transfigured in mirrors
in the halls of the surrealist escapist
monk. Fleeing dreams, and harmony
is the only link, the theoretical prayer.
    (Art lost in itself. the metaphysics
    of frustration, which is not to say
    despair. Orchestration, a game of logic
    to dispel confusion, which is
    madness, as the only defense . . . ,

Now a maze, now a highway, a delicate
dance, a fencing-match at the boundary
of probability. Control of intellect,
(like the Cyclops trembling in fear at a too-gentle touch,)
to be graceful enough to surprise the world in an awkward
pose.
    (This precise dance. Dangerous
    as it is, it does not imply
    strength for the attack, precarious
    with guilt. The epithet,
    shouted, "Absurd.")

by CRAIG PRESSON, University of Arkansas

LABYRINTH

Cool and slipp'ry you go dripping
down my mind
etching out your wand'ring ways;

And I oblige and slip behind you
        with my eye
    Casually watching blind
        meand'rings
    drawn by cool unhurried movement
'Til, on turning, I am frightened
    by the power of your maze.

             by EVY ALBERT, University of Florida

A lizard's eye shuts

(the first snows rise
toward me from a shallow sky.
through seared leaves cold earth
thrusts me into winds
that stoop with heavy cold.
I plunge into the sky,
earth heavy on my back.
the lizard with the frosted
bones is sopping up
what's left of sunlight
—selfishly because I too
fear the cricket's warning.
now the last leaves rise
from branches almost bare
and the lizard on the stone
warms its dragon blood
—alone though I too
have felt my spine
hooked on the owl's night.

this fall is endless
the snows rise
I sink under
the earth's heavy foot.
some woman's whisper
feeding my visceral embers)

and opens.

by FREDERICK CHIRIBOGA, Madison College, Va.

SONG OF THE STEPPENWOLF

Frozen sky of ink, indelible pole of the pale moon,
    waning in the death grasp of time.

The grass parts like icy shafts of insipid light
    forced to break rather than bend.

East, ever eastward in the Drangnach Ostend, across
    the face of Europe, the true face, the earth.

Nostrils aflame with barbed air, piercing the lungs
    deep in the vitals,

Sinews, limber in the night, warmed by their own
    heated motion,

Fire in the entrails, a consuming ice of a fire
    which Prometheusly burns.

Wings across the moon, a hunter delivers death with
    fierce talons, to a mute roaring in the face of death.

Stars wink at the irony; the moon travels on like
    a travelling band—wearily.

Ghostly the wind moves across knolls, the grass,
    winging the scent of life's pretender,

Aware in a second—silence; weeping fire-flash;
    water on the entrail fire; vapor.

Of five, two remain. Faintly man's laughter, the
    carrion's call, floats and victorious Diana flies.

by **GARY A. RICHARDSON, Northeast Louisiana State University**

THE HURRICANE

When the wind claimed its death
    he took a little of all of us
Some a home
        or our own

Like a giant hand
        upon the land.

Maybe it is our reward
    for progress
        pollution
        and electric wonder.

by **EDWARD R. THATCHER, Louisiana State University**

SEASONING

The whetted wind, harsh winter's coarse incisor,
Carves mortal meat, that mutton men call man.
Then forked flow of blowing fallen snow
Examines man with pointed punctures deep.
The sleeted spit still turns, the fat to whittle,
On frozen fire, the dainty art of frost.
And man, his meathead cold, unconscious, gropes
Home safely, heated haven for his hopes.

When April fools hoot halt to weeks of marching
They also end fermenting of the fruit.
Stewed man can leave his pressure cookered can
To rinse in cloudy faucets' showers sweet.
Thus cleaned he sits awaiting to be served
In traffic salads or financial soups.
And man, tomatohead, unconscious, rolls,
Refrigerated, home; diluted goals.

On summer days the Baker's ovens cook
The floury pulp of people unprotected.
Then kneads that bread, adds gust of dusty powder,
Soft boils in greasy sweat and then repeats.
Next, smoking wind, earth's furnace rolling pin,
Begins to blow its breath of pale prostration.
And man, his doughhead hot, unconscious, crawls
Home stumbling into crumbling, melting walls.

When August ovens ban their banal bake,
And close their doors before the wintry wake,
It's time for men to keep those shells from harm
Which shield the greyish meat from frozen germ,
For soon the winter will attempt to crack
With hammer hail and frost his brittle sack.
And man, his nuthead whole, unconscious, falls,
From pagan paws, through air, to sacred stalls.

by **DANIEL A. WELLS, Duke University, N. C.**

BOOK OF THE DEAD

asteroid-outside
all in a word
spinning to start
bigbang do it over

77

apart & not grasping
deadening motion
we have no words
to hail aeneas

i'm sorry the arsehole's
the ego's unloosening
chokes vocabulary
let it die let the

nothing is sometimes
deadening motion
riddle's conundrum
confuse your confessor

asteroi-outside
your dead reason is

    for this
        definitions

circumlocution
lost in a vacuum
starting to spin
small wheel again

unwanted alone
deadly still
lost in a vacuum
bring back the dead

clogged up in rimes
tightening rein
riddles the plain
let it go die, then

lost in a vacuum
deadly still
lockt in a punpun
it is all ABSTRACT

world times nine
you were betrayed

by NOEL DAVID FINNEY, Old Dominion University, Va.

I ASK FOR SILENCE, ALSO

i ask for silence, also
as did Neruda, the father of the love that a
small brown bird carries in his eyes

to be able to grow with the sun's music
and to care for the newborn of the shells
to ride with the warm blood of the fields
and to greet the aged word
which falls from a flower near its birth of death
to enter a room
which does not quarrel with the truth
that love often forgets

i long for more
but they will come
as i sleep in the bed that grows
from the children of time

i thank all friends
with an offering of love, which rises
from the leaves of my breast

79

i will not be alone
for i will have with me
my mother silence, who will lead me by the hand
down the long path
where my feet will be kissed with the joy
that walks with a tender voice of the stone

i will pray for the roots
to grow from my heart and drink from the river
where i may be
beside the soft face of the lark
the lark may teach me his soul
and i will weep for the kindness of the light
that brings me unto him

i will stand alone
and know the cloud's sorrow
as it is carried in the hands of the wind
i will find everywhere of everything
as i breathe the breath given from the bush
in this land my eyes will grow from the blossoms of the trees
and i will leave my eyes in the breast of night
that the moon may kneel over them
and show me the moving arms of spring

i may then rise to greet the mountain

i have asked for silence also,
with a tongue that lies still
but wishes to grow with the earth

by ALAN BRITT, University of Tampa, Fla.

AFTER

After
I shut the water off
silence
hangs at the windows like curtains.

The candle
eats circles out of the black.
Water.   Faucet.   Spigot.
One drop
hangs
like a transparent pear
ripening.
Elongated neck.
Ripening.
It falls
a clear circle
breaks open the night.
Past the sink
past the floor
past the earth
to a core I can neither see nor hear,
it may go further
changing shapes,
but while I watch
it only drips
and is gone.

by SHEILA HOPE JURNAK, Tulane University, La.

THE DEATH OF AN ARTIST

The strong, sweet smell of alcohol
Hung around his long death
Like a swinging votive candle
Keeping watch,

Flittering, fluttering, giving him,
Now and then,
A glimmer of peace
But more often lighting his way to hell.

Two were there when he died,
A priest, whom he raged and ranted at,
Not of his Faith, but faithful,
And a woman with tired eyes
Who loved him.

He was an artist who could paint the black soul of the devil
On canvas,
Or his estranged father,
Whom he loved but could not please,
Nor could he get him out of his being.

Three were there, when he died;
Father Joe, with a penitent face,
A woman, who loved him, kerchief tied around her head
Like a blue madonna,
And his absconding Papa, a sporadic ghost.

Three were there when he died,
Those he denied,
But loved in his way,
A remnant of those who had loved him.

Three were there—

by EVELYN ZDROJEWSKI, West Virginia State College

JONATHAN EDWARDS AROUSED MY KIN

Jonathan Edwards sleeps by me,
heatedly beats me painfully pale.
Hell sounds awe my feigned deaf ears.

I strip off sheet in winter heat.
Ancestral grief grips again,
even though I sanely swear

that I choked hell dead in smoke
from cross fire sparked in my mind.
Fanatical kin arise to sing

hellacious hymns to scarlet soul
of bitter fire, with silent scream.
Oh Jonathan, I fear their fear.

in ironic dreams that ridicule sleep.
I wake to preach sermon of sense,
merely charred from sleepless sleep.

by MARGARET HORNE STEINER, Madison College, Va.

SCOOP SALT AND CARRY SAND

Fit joints and tighten bolts, for time is passing by.
Each pawn takes part. Conveyers move relentlessly.
Ideas spring into men's heads, but foremen cry,
"Don't think! Just work! That is what you're paid for, see?"

Add parts and polish chrome, for orders are behind.
Hands work, not brains. Baboons could handle this career.
For many, while limbs labor, daydreams fill the mind,
But others' minds are void. Their souls are dead, I fear.

Wash cups and wipe lipstick, for working days will end.
Each man work hard. Some pawns are sacrificed,
Since automation is the corporation's friend.
Machines' work, without overtime, is lower priced.

Scoop salt and carry sand, advancement is a must.
Few men succeed, for robots don't make managers,
But daydreamers with vital souls arrive or bust.
Few pawns make queen. Success and dull men are strangers.

by TIMOTHY L. BOND, Salem College, W. Va.

CANTATA OF THE LIVING DEAD

Movement I: Life

The panting hart seeks the watering place
    while the torrid wind wears a fiery face;
    the limitless cold and dark of space
    calls out to man to forsake this race
    of passion and error and deadly embrace.
The new birth on the eastward hill
    will multiply to an arid still
    and parch and wither the cumbered quill
    that seeks the cool of a shaded mill
    of melted metal, to drink his fill.
God wears a grimace, a ferrous head,
    that fills all the earth with heat and dread;
    man turns away to kill the dead
    in suicidal sickness that poisons his bread.
    in aluminum tunics and sandals of lead.
    Yet we seek the dimension that angels tread
When will you be still, God, and cool your hand?
    When will you let coolness cover the land?
    When will you destroy the hot, bloody band
    that ties up this package of smoking soot-sand
    and splits the spirit between blaring and bland?
    When will you be still, God, and ease your hand?
When will you be still, man, and stop the crime,
    the rape of the Earth, your Mother sublime,
    the murder of Man, your Brother divine,
    the blaspheme of Honor, both your and mine?
    when will you be still? Will it be in time?

Movement II: Life

How does the mind lessen its pace?
Where does the heart find its place?

Green screams through dreams of light,
rosy hues grow purple bright
in the night of blackest passion.

84

Is it here
in the tall lamps and milkcans that fashion
a city of night dreams and day fears
that mind might mend or the heart ration
its strangling, caressing tears?

Gently bursting bubbles of aqueous gleam
silently glide,
while the pale-faced bride,
the yellow monster,
watches, waiting, the slow and terrifying
descent of my golden fantasy,
jealously beckons me
break
my contemplation.

. . . .

The cold light of August broke forth
on the wretched, rotting body,
once inhabited by a soul,
now gored with degeneration
and the gangrenous reincarnation
of death

Movement III: Life

When death takes a man by the hand
and leads him to that silken land
where sweet and smooth like slipping sand
dreams slink past on silken strand,

Why do we mortals moan and weep
(secretly longing for that soft sleep)?
We cry for ourselves, and for our deep
resistance to fate. Because we must keep

The faith with reality. We must remain
until death comes again and again and again.
. . . And then, no more.

by PRISCILLA HUNTER ROACH, Louisiana State University

RITA

Hair,
Black as the night of moonless gloom.
Lips as pressed with a hot iron.
Body movements coordinated as the sounds of Bird Man,
Bronze as copper-tin mixed,
As titillating as her name,
Rita.

by NATHANIEL P. CHIZER, Dillard University, La.

APRIL 14, 1966

Batman swings and heroes through
    Our chevrolet-ford world;
Mr. clean stands like a monster
    Of rhodes and rules like ajax;
Tinsel, foot-worn sphere, reeking
    Of jade-east from new york,
Lay down your transparent laurels
    To rest in a sepulcher,
Push back the patio gate of non-
    Rustable aluminum and relive,
Escape the dirty drain of unforseen
    Dreams to the reality of vanishing
Time that must be washed clean
    With new-found elbow-grease.

by CLAUDIA D. THOMPSON, University of South Carolina

BEDROOM SCENES

1

street light and light from the conquered moon
synthesize
and Moog music and perfumed air spray
empty the darkness
like blood from a soldier's wound

2

miniature atomic puffs
spread out from smiles
polluting the atmosphere
and sitar sounds drone
and synthetic serenity
everywhere drools from bottles
like blood from some soldier's wound

3

stick man in the corner
hunches up heroically
like a praying mantis
anticipating execution
in Love's desperate orgasm
like blood that spurts from a soldier's wound

by VINCENT B. LEITCH, University of Florida

SECOND SONNET

My pug-nose you, who for a year
Of dogwood blooms and blind typhoons
Have been, throughout, my dearest dear,
Who stood the pain of awful tunes
(Ravel, d'Indy did not mind you!),

Without your scherzo gab, complete
With devil's grin or moral hue,
Past weeks had been a marble fleet.
Andante! Sweeping like this planet, time,
That tossed our thoughts together, strides between
Us now, and forking streams so long foreseen
Will glide us, gently split, to our own rhyme;
Like melodies of point and counter point estranged,
We swirl, pursuing harmonies not yet arranged.

by KENNETH ROYCE HUGGINS, West Georgia College

TO RICHARD M. NIXON

How can you sleep
With so much fresh blood
Rushing through your thoughts?
Baptizing in tropical rains
Of distant Thailand
Didn't wash the blood away,
Or stop the new-poured
Daily gallons;
But, you slept quietly in Thailand.
The mechanical heart pumps
Blood, that is no longer
Your blood, through the brain,
Electrifying headline images of
Tomorrow's new supply . . .
    And yet you sleep—
    And how you sleep—
    And undisturbed you sleep—
The hearts beat,
The blood pumps,
The bayonets rip,
The blood flows.
You sleep.

The blood flows,
Streaming into creeks,
Into Eastern rivers,
To become your blood stream
While you sleep.

by DENNIS SCHUETZ, West Virginia University

THE SOCIETY OF JESUS

(This poem is written for great Jesuits—for Hop-
kins and Teilhard and Ignatius Loyola, who are
dead; for Francisco Ornelas and Natio, who are
still living; and for Jesus Christ, who some say is
also still alive.)

Bent-kneed Ignatians,
Followers of this
Soldier turned Jesus-
        lover,
Lead, striding upright,
The Jesuit,
The bold-blaze way,
Slicing holes,
Fiercely slashing, gashing
The body of darkness,
Effectually killing heresy
or Worse—complacency
With brutal, steely,
Not merely contemporary,
But forever truth,
Baptizing in its bleeding
        Death
Our bloody Birth.
From satisfaction's womb
They eject us—
        kicking, crying,

But truth-taught we can't but live,
Embarking—Is it
On a brick wall or
On a rock road to
Magnificent, munificent Majesty
Of a sort
Worth the often bruising
Brutal—never brutalizing—bout,
Not fisticuffs
But warring with
Dark, dank, death-dealing
Fear-unknowing?
They deal life-blows,
Inflict immortal wounds,
Naming Jesu as the
Sole hope of healing.
Lord, these men—
Long-taught, truth-tall
Men—wage commitment
Fiercely
Dealing not in compromise,
Peaceful negotiation,
Placation on wobbly knees,
All a-stutter,
But in unqualification,
In total acts—
    Complete surrender
Uninsured, non-guaranteed,
Not-less-total victory wins.

All you—those born and not yet dead,
Let us go loving and
Laughing the way through.

This business of living
Is breathing laughter in lieu of air,
Is pat-a-pat of tears falling, not mere thumping
    muscle driving blood faithfully forever—
      So it seems,

Is wide eyes, wide smile, wide awake,
Is expansive *being,*
Is dreadful bursting germination,
Is me-making, you-loving,
Is constant variation, perpetual new.

Living is demanding me;
Living is pushing me jerkily, bewilderingly somehow up.
Acquiring knowledge in hope of
      Reaching Wisdom,
I laugh broadly, ache only largely,
        And walk.

         by JUDITH M. BAILEY, Louisiana State University

SEA SCAPE

White horses
splashing relics from another world
another time
upon yesterday's mountains
bearing weight of outcast shells inanimate;
Sandy dunes
winding to another same
tomorrow
building mountains crystalline
guide mother turtle to her sandy nest.

         by ED BAKER III, Elon College, N. C.

R.S.V.P.

Oh take me in
Sweet jesus
deliver my soul
asphyxiated by defeat—
I must retreat
this second thought
you have bought
a repenter
not a sinner

to a midnight dinner
of disgust and lust
red ripe passions of pleasure
will savour our tongues
oh sweet jesus
may I bring a friend
to dinner.

by TIM HOGAN, Murray State College, Va.

LOVE POEM NUMBER ONE

The arms of my woman, wrapped 'round me tightly,
Now hurt my enveloped torso
As my bare chest gasps beneath her breasts,
Struggling to breathe beneath her weight

But it matters not; the pain of her body
Pressed against mine is dwarfed by the pleasant
Memories of the fusion of the night,
And we rise and fall in tortured harmony

We died in darkness, gave up our ghost in slumber,
Only to be born again 'mid streaming light
Of April's reincarnate roots
Piercing our dualistic solitude

Once was I a boy with notions in my head
Of what grass-greenness tasted like
And the sound made by the roaring of the sky
When the earth is held against the ear

Once was I lost in beauty's realm, unable
To descend to morbid dreams of mortal fears;
Once did my hands hold the rainbow's shades
And see the secret of the river's liquid life

Then was I alive, and wept I then for the Christ
That is yet to ring out the goodness of man,
And my tears flowed with the blood of all our wounds
Until it became the milk of Paradise

On such was I nurtured, but I lost the way
Of love and life, and the harpies of this world
Chained me to futile fears, and I had to
Die with my woman to soar again to pale-blue life

And so I have crossed the world from Jerusalem
And emerged atop the mountain of Byzantium,
My head spinning amid the swirl
Of the sacred zephyrs of infinity

Eternal am I now, and endless is my realm of love
That my finite woman has bequeathed to me
As a remnant of the dying of the night
And the awakening of our sun-seeing souls

by DAVID MILLER, University of Florida in Gainesville

WELCOME HOME, BROTHER

Little crooked man
Bent in the sidewalk,
His tire legs hot.
An empty pencil box,
Red swollen eyes
Lying deep and thoughtless . . .
Trying to remember those cooler days,
Down the river . . .
The dust from the cotton
Melted by the damp river breeze . . .
Youth, yes young eyes
Strong, meaningful, dark . . .
A panther's legs . . . powerful, sleek.
A hazy sun rolled the sweat
Down his back . . . the breeze soaked it up.
Arms that drove an 18 lb. sledge
Hold an empty pencil box.
That love for his country
That love to save a life
That love took his legs . . .
And gave him memories . . .
Welcome home, brother.

by J. CREIGHTON MICHAEL, University of Tennessee

DUSKDREAM

evenings,
the easy trees
stand off a high weeping skybrow:
every blade every lilting heartsung
leaf language seems somewhom strange,
so that i never know if
the leaky sun or i am speaking,

or if we two both are making
some giggling symphony
between ourselves.
slowthroated, the riversmelling
dusk devours with the awful mouths
of shadowcats who come writhing
hugely up our street.
the leaves are filled with children,
whose such one green voice
makes me wonder whether
they are children at all,
or whether maybe the girlish air
has spawned other dancers,
the real ones, whose cries
like shrouds lift into orbits
of amber, remember other evenings
when the bruised rain escaped
unmourned and answerless,
when the only answer was
in my blood and life
solved itself.
familiar with purple damask,
the first-fingered twilight
knows the rythm of upswept stars,
breathes like an Amazon
through vacant lots in want
and caught trees standing trampish
in sorrow, one arm lifted.
now, soon, darkness will answer me
with new mysteries of her own,
serene, without comment or question,
because there are none,
no small boy even to break the
seating stillness with a shout.

by STEPHEN BECHTEL, Greenville College, N. C.

JUST LEAVES

I knew it would be a cold day today.
I looked through my window last night
and the leaves rustled the onslaught
of autumn and fell dead to an early frost.
They called at my window to come in;
or was it for me to come out?
I rode my idea of that cold day
on a doomed brown leaf that fell
under a speckled autumn moon.
A friend fell today like
a doomed brown leaf in an early frost.
Should I stay in or go out?
A leaf falls and friends have fallen
and I knew it would be a cold day today.

by JONATHAN RUDGE, Morris Harvey College, W. Va.

I like to think about
your smile
and the way your eyes
grow soft with
understanding.
If time should deny
some part of you
from memory
your eyes will always
remain.

by BETH EVANS, Warren Wilson College, N. C.

KIGO

spring

An ivy climbs my wall,
clutching at the smooth grey stone
with small green fingers.

A dew-flecked jonquil
nods to the sun and flaunts
her crown of brilliants.

Long days must be near:
the melons on my neighbor's fence
are beginning to swell.

summer

The old bay dozes
basking its sleep-smoothed face
in the warm sun.

A willow idles
on the bank, letting her hair
trail in the water.

I ride on quiet
water, below and above
the star-dotted sky.

Feathers of dust rise
from the creaking cart wheels.
The sun is small and white.

Does the cicada
outside my window think he
is lulling me to sleep?

The sun sinks lower:
now only topmost branches
are still touched with light.

autumn

Two rustling birches
touch branches—old gossips
whispering together.

The heavy round moon
climbs slowly—my plate
lies unnoticed.

Invisible hands
seize and scatter withered leaves,
tease the old yardman.

  The ocean shrugs,
trying to flick the little boats
from its broad back.

The naked tree flails
its thin arms, straining to catch
the fleeing crescent.

winter

The morning is white.
To the bare black twigs
fine flakes are clinging.

On the bare sweep
of new snow—my footprints
and a rabbit's.

Outside ice owns all.
Even the thin bright sunlight
looks cold and brittle.

A small grey bird lights
on the snow; in his beak is
a yellow kernel.

spring

At the edge of snow—
an impatient violet
called by the sun.

An ivy climbs my wall,
clutching at the smooth grey stone
with small green fingers.

by MARGARET CHARLET, Francis Nicholls State College, La.

The morning woke only to find itself smothered in clouds.
Taken in by sleepy eyes peering through windows streaked
with dirt—a half life begins anew.
Countless rows of winter weary houses answer
the dawn with paint chipped silence.
High in the naked oak a robin home too early refuses to sing.
Below, the soft crunch of frozen snow betrays the
padded feet of a loner searching for breakfast
And down the road a ton of cold steel cries one last protest
as it shakes to life.

Bare feet hurry across the cold floor and retreat to
the warmth of an electric blanket.
What else can you do when the world doesn't realize
April has come?

by BILL GIBSON, Roanoke College, Va.

THE SOUL AND THE BODY

The thoughtful rainwarm thumping of the heart
In panoply of crackling fired crystal,
Vibrates through the planes of light and light
Creating lightening without fire, warmth and great desire.

Energy in formless vapor fills with light
And shifts without direction, feels
The rhythm of the longing in the crystal's interstices,
Pulses, glows, involves itself in warmth and seeks
expression.

The images of rainwarm motion flicker
Through the fields of matter, find new forms
And different channels and fill the fallow
Paths of senses with the warmth and great desire.

The moving image finds attraction, leaps the
Limits of the senses into space as ultimate as
Entropy, is lost without relation 'til there comes
Rainwarm vibration and the image of a crystal.

by WALTER MILLS, Old Dominion University, Va.

A snowy Saturday
And up the rusty fire escape
To Warren and Jay
Calling from above
From the unlit theatre
From the open door
With steamy breath and shakes
With Warren's nasal, biting but
Friendly just the same calling my name
And Jay
Fat, placid, liver-lips Jay

Closing the door
As I climb the snow-ridged iron steps
Avoiding the icy rail climb
Quickly to the now open door
To the welcome watery eyes of Jay
To Warren's shot fond
Morning Bastard
To the theatre gray in the winter morning.

The old theatre in Robinson Hall
With wooden seats in sets of four
Still to be broken to their evening rows
Yielding to scents of
Cheap pine and painted canvas
To coke cups indifferently supporting damp
Tobacco snakes within.
Haunted by the pink-gel light of evenings
The orchestra six piece full
Stein faces charcoaled, with
Blue liner.
Red plastic glow over doors
I watch Warren and Jay
Wandering in the stage-musty light
Like young priests
Searching their father's tomb
They are the Wasp child the morning he sees not
The shimmering cobweb of light
But branches, colored bulbs held together by
Hooks and wires.
And like the child
They will lie under
Staring straight up into the forest of
Green nettles
Electric blues, greens, yellows
Some, warm on the flesh,
Some pinpoints barely seen.
Warren sawing an adenoid tune
Jay rolling beside
The professor and his butler

Marionettes triggering their own strings
In the madness of the second verse
Their shadows still haunting the flies

Now the panting, sweat, wiping forehead,
Warren short of his Lorrilard breath
With the sound of a slow car on snow
Passing by beneath.
Ask about dinner at Lou's
(We'd see the only waitress in Hanover
Whose smile could thrill us to tip.)
Agreed
We leave by the house back door
Down the steps
Past posters
Over tile we pass
Through the double wind-lock doors
Onto icy sidewalks and snow
Sunlit snow, heaped all around.

by **RICHARD DOUGLASS, Vanderbilt University, Tenn.**

THE SCHOLAR

He admired the French.
He read the Greeks although a great author he was
In his own right. (*An Explanatory Treatise of English Tea*
Won him world renown.)
Of course, he did not believe in God—he could not, he said:
He was educated.

He was a respected man.
His dress influenced the mode of the time.
He traveled far and wide, lecturing constantly, and
His elocution was often imitated.
The other day he made his longest trip.
He went to Hell.

by **THOMAS C. WALLACE, Marshall University, Va.**

THE RECIPIENT

And in the time of the judges there was no king;
    Great was the need for unity and cooperation.
Rays of sin shone on everything
    While corrupted man did what pleased him most.
A laughing God looked down on him
    When he thought himself omnipotent;
For he who had received great gifts
    Could not remember the giver.

Now there is a great monarchy,
    Law to rule and conscience to guide.
Rays of sin shine on everything
    While man tries to reflect the bad.
When the mirror of his will breaks,
    He again feels himself omnipotent;
For he who has received great gifts
    Cannot remember the giver.

by ALICE CLAY WEST, University of Miami, Fla.

APPLE TREE

A tiny, brown seed sown at random
In the dark brown earth,
Pushes finally to rough black height,
Shooting its rambling branches
Into the blue-green country void
Near a rain-rutted, dusty lane
That forsakes the hard-hearted city
And snakes towards the soft-bellied land.

From stark limbs peek hints of fingers
That ball into small, hard fists
Of green that multiply and incline with time
To dangling orbs of lusty red,

103

Destined for one of several fates:
To lose their grip while green
And never know their prime;
To feel the tender palm of some rural lass,
Fill the splintered space of a rustic pail
And bounce on Firestone wheels to market;
Or, clinging too long to their source,
Rot in the still air of their birth,
Knowing no purpose but to be and not to be;
Or, at the whim of some chance gust,
Fall upon the dewy meadow not to rise again;
Or, if the land is dry, roll with abandon
Down the clovered hill into the charging stream
And sail away to die in some unknown place;
Or halt upon the water's margin
To await the deadly frost.

But still stands that lonely tree
Upon the naked, wintry hill—
Passing nearby along the frozen lane,
We watch its icy arms brave the biting breeze,
We have faith that another season
Shall find the tree resplendent again
And proud in its emerald-ruby robe.

by ASA PASCHAL, University of North Carolina

Solemned by the silent
emptiness of the
approaching night,
A wave of darkness surrounds
the dancers—
halting their merry
Carousel.

Hoping to awaken new life,
      the wind gusts with
            overwhelming strength;
But, alas, failure,
      for the night rules all.

Serene and undisturbed by
      assaults made by the wind in
            moments of despair,
He engulfs life with folds
      of shadow.
As he travels about the last
      breath of life is swept
            away,
And he is the victor.
Tranquility dominates his manner—
      he rules all

The wind in his domain
      stubbornly rebukes the night,
Casting leaves hither to with
      resounding gusts.
Blown out, the threatener dies;
And the darkness falls.

The night rules all.

by CAROL STALEY, University of Miami, Fla.

III. AMBER WAVES OF GRAIN
(In concern for the American Legion credo)

It is not faith that holds the deadly gun
Not faith that holds the gun
Nor hope that fires it.

Alone.
All day, through the night,
And there is no relief.
There is nothing below the rising mists
Nothing above the rising mists
Nothing above or below.
Even yesterday holds no refuge
For the sticky thoughts that plague his shattered mind
And there is no relief.

O flag!
O proud and honored flag!
Rippling in the sickening breath
Of anguish and death
Of dissension
Of anguish and death

My country 'tis of thee
Sweet land of liberty

And death.

Think not of death
Think not of death and needless wars.

My country 'tis of thee
Sweet land of liberty

Does he lift his weary eyes?
Does he lift his blood-soaked eyes?
A feeble glance cannot reveal the rising spirit
Which slowly glides away.
He cannot see.
Goodbye, goodbye, goodbye

Sweet land of liberty
Of thee we sing.

by KEN BRADLEY, University of Virginia

106

I want and want
until wanting
fills the empty spaces
but underneath
there are still traces
of something missing.

It lies there lost
under the table
in my memory
like missing pieces
of a picture puzzle.

I look and search
to find them:
the pieces of times
that are lost.

But I don't have a flashlight.

Only hope saves.

by LIZABETH LEVKOFF, Newcomb College, La.

ON THE 100th ANNIVERSARY OF THE BIRTH OF MAHATMA GANDHI
10-2-69

One pallid afternoon
Mahatma left our shore
Setting foot
In a swift boat rowing up
The river of glory.

He is for ever and ever gone
In his river of glory.

Oh Lord! among the ashes of the dead,
Pick up his
And rain them back to us,
To fertilize the hearts
Of men of good will.

We need him on this side of the shore!

by **JOSEPH E. PENTE, Louisiana State University**

GIFTS FOR PRIESTS ON FATHER'S DAY

Rexall Drugs has on display
GIFTS FOR PRIESTS ON FATHER'S DAY:

A papal bucket that in a minute
Blesses whatever you put in it,

A pocket-flask for two and a quarter
Holds a pint of bonded "holy water,"

Indulgences, gained standing or kneeling
With free bromos for that stuffy feeling,

Bees-wax candles that inspire contrition
Or obtain, toute de suite, the wildest petition,

Plaques depicting, "The Garden of Eden"
Once unobtainable outside of Sweden,

For a statue that'll knock them dead,
See the one of St. Denis . . . decapitated,

Pious cards—not the Hallmark trash—
Inscribed with verses by Ogden Nash,

There's a carillon with bells that chime
"Get me to the church on time,"

A confessional that's a sure corrector
Equipped with the latest lie-detector,

Oils and relics for incurable ills
Why waste the inheritance on doctor bills?

Restroom fixtures designed with flair
W.C.'s modeled on St. Peter's Chair,

A baptismal font—a profound submerger
And with it a Coastguard life preserver,

Guitars and drums for the hippy mass
And a beaded vestment that's a gas,

There are holy breads for little shavers
In Jello's six delicious flavors,

Other items for church and home
Are available for the man of Rome,

But to really delight the celibate
See Rexall's agents from Computa-Date.

      by GERALD GROVES, University of South Carolina

BALLOON MAGIC

The balloon man
     in scarred blackness and
     muffling overcoat tucked
     close to rain cold ears
a shadow within the dirt of city night's
fogged neon.

And above all his peasant sameness, his
balloons!
   red and blue, striped and plain
  they attack the sky darkness and
ask for me.

  I ask his name.
    a red balloon answers me and he
    snatches my quarter with a
    slow stretching smile
  Rain Falls
I run from it but he stays
   under the sky. Wondering,
    I look up to see his balloons!
 red and blue, striped and plain
They are his umbrella.
   I understand and
smile back at him.

   Quietly happy
    he has given me a
    small piece of his
 happiness—
    a balloon!
But it is enough,
    now we are both
 Balloon Protected
against the rain and
  the lonely, neon
    streaked night.

    by CYNDY KERCOUDE, Roanoke College, Va.

A slap from the wind, and a break,
and three kingdoms,
ancient, saprophyte, or mine,
launched in pain,
tumble like merchant Eve
or Thomas a Beckett,
flutter like butterflies
die in the wind,
life palisaded, and drying;
brittle, lost keel
swinging pendulum
beating the anvil
that forges time that pulls
like a dragging anchor—
Gyred, swirling,
until upon
the moldy forest loam
the leaf rests.

by RICHARD NILSEN, Guilford College, N. C.

CONSECRATION
(Military Peepshow)

The linted lion moves across
The well-tiled floor red with the blood
Of the skin-nosed ragged gladiators. He moves,

Searching out the ink-stained hands,
Images of Christ beside the fountain
Ripped into a myriad of well-whipped fragments.

Stinking does he move,
Stinking, stinking!

111

Stinking with the oatmealed death of the opposition
He moves,
    having heard his name called with triumph,
      his mane wiped clean with frightened silence.

      He moves with the blood glistening
      Upon his skin streaked with screams.

by ALAN DAVIS, University of Southwestern Louisiana

when the grass has turned brown
when the grass is weeds dying

when legs have forgotten crying
skirts put on for town

then will sound come sighing
then will leaves come down

then will legs pursue like hounds
then will bindings come unbound

weeds retreat
round repeat

by LYNNE HILLABRANT, Miami-Dade Junior College, Fla.

I REMEMBER

I remember how
    we lived in a one room shack
And how she pulled
    a cotton sack on her back

112

I remember how
    she would become ill
Working from sun up to
    sun down in a cotton field.

I remember watching her
    on her knees
Waiting to answer that
    white woman's needs.

I remember her
    scrubbing his floors,
Then having to go
    through his back door.

I remember how
    she used to pray
When she would come
    home from work every day.

I remember the
    day she died,
The night
    I cried.

I remember standing
    over her grave
Promising I would
    never live as a slave.

I remember how
    it was to be a nobody,
That's why tomorrow
    I'm gonna be Somebody.

by EDWARD E. RUCKER, Dillard University, La.

THE DIRTY JOKE

Jovial swans honk in prurient mirth
As the lover of Leda, detailed without dearth,
Slaveringly leers his tale through a beak
That a short while past her nape did seek.
Her nape he found, he lewdly chortled,
And with his strange heart on her breast, immortal
Zeus-swan aroused her with adroit pinions
Smirking smugly, her loosening thighs his dominion.
"An egg then oozed from her womb," he screeched,
"Attesting to my potency and her vaginal reach."
Sated, both by thoughts of Leda and webbed cronies,
He became Hera's lord, blind to his hatching patrimony.

by ALAN JOHNS, Wofford College, S. C.

STONE GARDEN

Stone and Steel rise to tower
Over the yielding earth,
Isolating rivers defying its birth.
A sigh, a smile, to thrust its power
Over warm creators who boast its worth.

Time is dumb to stare or try to wear
Away the autographs, tears, and lives,
That pierce the earth with knives
Of steel and stone. To lend a care
To rules of games that have no prize

Compels the weed to spare the flower;
Forces the ant to sing out its mirth,
While marching past the life that bears
All hope, all dreams to a house that dwarfs its size;
To make the keeper pile up stones to form a prayer.

by CLEO LANCASTER, Elizabeth City State University, N. C.

PROGRESS AND PERDITION

The days of sun and peace are gone
and times of curiosity,
when intuition was so strong
when we could hear and feel and see.
The evening of Christ's Church and man
is tawdry glass from crystal sand.

The days of sun and peace are gone
and cold dank winds of knowledge chill
the alabaster mold of dawn
that was warmed by Promethean will.
The evening of Christ's Church and man
is tawdry glass from crystal sand.

The days of sun and peace are gone—
ecstatic prophets used to roam
who shared and spoke in tongues and song
without dogma, spire, or dome.
The evening of Christ's Church and man
is tawdry glass from crystal sand.

The days of sun and peace are gone.
Children's love and mysticism
are fading now and being drawn
to baser briefcase erudition.
The evening of Christ's Church and man
is tawdry glass from crystal sand.

by C. R. MEYERS III, Davis & Elkins College, W. Va.

I

    rise up early in the morning
and fall down
        crawl awhile
        before I can see
flowers and trees growing in muddy streets
of gold's mother country
           I
          reach out
                with would be
gratitude, against
          long forgotten
         clouds blowing
in my early morning's sunset shadows
        among
            dictatorial
                faces
         pushing them
              I crawl . . . .

I

cry on silvery eagles
        guarding
     nameless figures
            above wooded tombs . . . .
      while god's little acre grows into my
                pocket's
       green staples; black pages
         caress
       white collars
      with concern
          for Berlin's Bridges
         about to topple.

           by HARRY MOON, Tulane University, La.

FRAGMENTS IN CHURCH
For Brian Walshe

"Go and tell Jesus you are very sorry,"
He's heard it all before and so have I.
How many years ago I knelt to ask
Which of my sniggering sins was mortal.

My mother said "I'd rather see my son
Inside his coffin than outside the church."
She said it like the old ancestral curse
It was.

At mass I thought of dirty books
And blushed as if the priest could read my thoughts,
Taking God's body, thinking of my own,
And eating to my own damnation.

"Sweet Saviour bless us ere we go"
On summer evenings when the later light
Revealed the flaking stone more likely plaster.
Old voices gently dragged through benediction,
The statues were innocuously bad;
Smiling Saint Patrick with his outsize shamrock,
Teresa with that nineteen-twenty look.
Familiar fakes and well-defined illusions.

In winter it was different.
I shuddered at the stretched anatomy
Of naked Christ dissected on the cross;
The glowing nightmare of the Sacred Heart
By candlelight lit up my sins.

The Virgin shone above in blue and white
With roses at her feet, the Mystical Rose,
Tower of Ivory and House of Gold.
The girl that scuffled in the local park
Could not be given such chivalric titles
And yet seemed just as unobtainable.
If both were lovers which of them proved false?

The children genuflect and tiptoe out,
Crossing themselves with taught, elaborate care.
I hear their lives begin outside the door.
"Go and tell Jesus you are very sorry."
I bow my head, I am a child again,
But much too old to cry.

by ANTHONY MORTIMER, Case Western Reserve University, Ohio

BUFFALOES ROAMING #2

Buffaloes roaming cacti-splattered fields
searching for mountain-foot grasslands.
Waterhole stops wash down sweat-glistened backs
and drops from black, fleshy snouts stain the ground.
Once again tireless hooves clomp—
Rusty valley walls scratching hot skies.
A cool breeze ruffles the herd's back
and horns raise to catch eyelids full.
Long tireless gazes across flat horizons,
changing horizons . . .
Female bellowings halt the herd,
defense circles take their instinct-guided forms.
Gasping, the female lies on her side—
pangs and oozings as the newborn slides out
and tumbles onto the prairie floor.
Burly head uplifted, the bull trots
back and forth along his posted herd—
the others watch, patiently.
The newborn struggles to unsteady feet—
slick-coated and dust encrusted.
In a few hours they will start,
A new mouth to be fed—
No grass.

by JAMES MAND, Wisconsin State University

SEED SICK

I hear by letter and rumor of your abortion,
And think back. Three years ago
We met and often talked through a wall
Over beer or coffee. Two years I watched
You work your life out in horror and tedious care,
Through three men children, and colors and shapes.
At your parties, beer in hand I scanned
The walls waiting for new abominations,
Vile vomitings in green, grey, and yellow,
Straight out of your mirror.
Or noted new work on a nude, a mutual acquaintance,
Put aside after an unalterable
Stroke across her thigh.

I learned later your earlier life:
A quick marriage, the first child followed
Fast by two more while living
In a log house with fire for light.
While your good mad man played
The graduate game one more year,
You bore the third boy. Hours daily
You sat alone on a mountain porch, your luxury,
Filling the hollow with banjo sound, keeping
Back the night.

Weary of a world of war,
Broken trying to reconcile Saigon
And his seminar in Spenser, your husband
Left it all, pulled out and moved
To another mountain town to take up teaching.
Two years I heard him daily damn
The war and curse man—arraign us all.
Those two years you turned from television's
Thursday death tally to answer your oldest
Son's first questions about God.

119

Infinitely unable to comprehend
Either finite insanity or infinite anything,
In pieces incapable of putting them together,
You painted madly, more often.

According to rumor or myth, one morning
Last spring, after a Dionysian
Weekend, a genuine sophomore
Brought your husband an apple in mischievous bribery,
Her trivial mind perverted by Milton's Genesis.
Mistaking stupidity for inspiration,
This time not at all aware,
He left with her and left you the core.

by HARRY BROWN, University of Ohio

CARVER

You are carved with definitive strokes
and patinated with the passing of years;
not unkindly, life chiseled you in hunks,
gave you character in your broad expanse of forehead,
heightened cheekbones, squared chin.
She has not scratched cross-hatched lines on you
or graven on you her intricate designs.
But sand-smoothed day by passing day,
you at sixty-three are lustrous to my touch
of hands that feel the fine edged lines
of your stone strong countenance.

by SISTER LOIS SHELTON, OSF, Marillac College, Mo.

TONKA

Iridescent hue,
Long, nectar seeking beak, and
Invisible whir
Of wings—the humming bird is
Nature's own helicopter.

The wary deer halts
As his sharp ear hears the step
Of the great hunter.
Motionless he stands, then, with
A flick of white tail, is gone.

Patiently she works,
Teaching, re-teaching a child.
Brow wrinkled, he thinks.
Concentration, then, the light—
Eyes shine! The teacher is paid.

by **RUTH ROSE, Marian College, Wis.**

THE DEPRESSION OF CARNIVALS

The depression of carnivals
that steams from flattened cups,
that cries from the screaming
ferris wheels that creep around
the sky—   behind

my father,
a showman in his time;
day after day in the haze of smoke
and in perfectly round spotlights
he would tell thousands of the wonders
of a glimpsed at world as if
he had written Genesis or could
with a word
spin all existence into catastrophe.

But now he can only direct
the passing of the salt
or expound upon the
failure of my mother
to stay a young woman,

his anger dead behind his eyes,
his head like an imperfect paper
weight held in my mother's hands,
his skin lepering into wrinkles
as the rain explodes the dust
off the rails of August porches—
in his broken, fragile whispers,
his desperate, vengeful whispers.

by THOMAS BAKER, University of Kentucky

SHELTER?

Long were the days of pain
I had spent within its walls,
And long were the nights of aloneness;
But who can depart from his pain
And his aloneness without regret?
It is not a garment I cast off this day,
But a skin that I tear with my own hands . . .
For to stay . . . is to freeze . . . and crystallize . . .
And be bound in a mould.

by SISTER DEBORAH, DC, Marillac College, Mo.

QUEEN OF THE MORNING

The wind burned a gentle warmth
into my cheek and I saw Dawn
smile in the tufted clouds above,
felt her soft breathing whisper
tender thoughts, fill the inner
realms of a hollowed heart.
Then she guided the pen
which etched words of deep
meaning for me to embrace
forever. Tiller of the heavens,
she reaped a golden harvest
and flung it across the
celestial arc for all to see
and to feel. But I knew
that my precious moments
with her would be brief, for
quickly and quietly as she
came she would depart,
seek new admirers beyond
the horizon.

by MARTHA HAYTER, University of Dubuque, Ia.

A STAINING OF THE MIND

> *Yet now despair itself is mild*
> *Even as the wind and waters are;*
> *I could lie down like a tired child*
> *And weep away the life of care*
> SHELLEY, 1818

Bysshe and his Mary
Love children
They had slipped away quietly

Off to the adventurous world
of each other
Mary had wished him more vulgar
Yet, what could surpass their
   ménage à trois and
   frequent deaths

Now
Young men with muscled thighs
are my lovers
Poets
They all waver and want
and still they're young men
their brides electric
their hair staunchly thick

I wanted one of you to take me
in the snow
Able to make exquisite love
Know that the heart of emotion lies not
in the brain, but rather with
your dark hands your long fingers that make
poems

I wanted a flower to talk to me
I wish one of you knew how to touch my back
Tried to ask you why you could not write
like Shelley
Build your words to open others
Come in late at night to show me
Lead me back and recite in your sleep

Leave
Take away your long curls
Your smooth shoulders
hard stomachs
I'm staying
Retreating with my roundness

Going to feed on my white skin
Untill one of you will learn
That I'm not asking to win
I'm only making all this noise
to maintain my dreams

by BONNIE KUSTNER, University of Iowa

INNOCENT

The curb hits me before I'm down
and I float in the gutter from image to image
as rivers run the lines of my face.
White, lamb
Red, fire
Black, stone.
Tears perform immersion as torn flesh supplies supper
and routines tumble from my mouth
in foreign prayer, pseudo-hoping
that the butterfly will leave my body.
But I know, not yet.
I must stumble more streets.

by LANA KIENAPFEL, University of Iowa

HANSON'S DOG (THE BEST OF ALL POSSIBLE WORLDS)

For Warren Slesinger

Sunday;
Worship;
Glorify the Lord and grace comes
Regular like autumn corn; (every autumn).

Hanson was in Church.
He was at One with God:
For an hour
He sang, and his spirit danced?
His feelings rose and fell with the word of the Lord?
He thought about death?
He thought about time?
He thought about God, and man, and kings of the world?
He though about breakfast after the Eucharist,
(the elements made his stomach gurgle),
He knew intuitively that he was hungry.
His food was not the food of gods.
It was eatING (futurific) that he was sure of.
(Well, I mean, everybody has to eat).

Hunger pleases me,
Sex pleases me,
Listening,
Watching,
Smelling,
Feeling pleases me;
Thinking pleases me, especially clear thinking,
And that's why I fail to attend and worship
At the Church and Faith of my choice.
Churching displeases me, (divinity student),
Because the arguments are weak.
(Whenever they are weak, pound the pulpit).
So I was up early, for a Sunday,
For me too,
Getting some breakfast food at
Kings,
Mkt.,
There wasn't much difference
Between me and Hanson then,
He was in Church, hungrily, thinking about Kings,
I was in Kings, hungrily thinking about God.
Only the setting was different;
His was stoic and proper,
Mine was stoic and improper;

I chuckled when I thought how clear it was
"That propriety is not meaningful in the light of Stoicism."

Anyway I chuckled and
Petted this dog—
(Hanson's dog)
Brown head,
Black body,
Flashy eyes,
Tail smartly wagging
In the air
Responding to my "Good Morrow,"
But most of All
Alive.—
On my way in the door of
Kings.
He might have been a dialectic dog,
I thought;
He might have thought
What a strange and sun-less-day it was,
He might have contemplated his tail,
Ferlinghtti's dog did;
He reminded me of a picture I had once seen of
Scott Buchanan,
Only without a cigarette,
But there was something dialectic about Hanson's dog—
Foolish—
I became irate
With myself,
Foolish to think of thinking dogs.
I picked up some eggs,
And looked out the seeing eye of Kings' window,
Smeared with the dried fly bodies
Of summer past,
Just at the moment
Hanson's dog flashed into the road,
Flipped a coin with a '61 Chevy,
And lost.

Hanson's dog was dead.
I didn't know Hanson,
And I'd never met his dog before,
But chances are, since I liked his dog
I'd like Hanson—
So I went out of Kings';
Grey day,
Walking normal,
Hands sweaty,
Cold,
and cursing,
Goddamn Stupid dog,
Goddamn Stupid dialectic dog,
Stupid Goddamn dog was bleeding from
His mouth, a big pool,
Steaming on the cold road,
From his bowels,
From his nose,
From his ears;
His eyes and tongue were all bugged out and
Dead.
It could have been Hanson,
Or me,
Or Leo T.,
Or anybody's Goddamn Universe
Come to an end.
The dog was needed;
Needed by Hanson,
Needed by me,
Needed by the '61 Chevy,
Needed by the dialectic,
Needed by Life.
It was dead.
I hope Hanson remembered his dog
In Church
To God
That day,
But I think he probably
Didn't take the Time,

Or just forgot.
He is Hungry.
I am Hungry,
But we aren't hungry for the same things.
I dragged Hanson's dog off the road.

by **ROBERT CAIN**, Olivet College, Mich.

ISAIAH

A gypsy out of Iowa,
you came to me, a weird

creature having more
ear rings than teeth.

This silver, strung
from your ears, tarnished

by your touch, and one
1939 Buick were all

you owned. You lived
in that dust—upholstered

backseat, napping at
nights with a cheesecloth

bedspread bound around
you, working during the day

laying the tarot cards
for others. You have travelled

all over Iowa for others,
yet, you remain the Hermit

flying across the Moon,
keeping your distance

from the crater sand, so
afraid of impact, so attracted

to the light that all
you could do was orbit.

You are still travelling.
Your teeth of black rot

tell your own fortune.

by VIRGINIA GILBERT, University of Iowa

ROCKING INTO NIGHT

Uncle Mal sat on the porch and rocked,
his chair creaking back and forth
across the cracks
of planks old and weathered,
stripped of their sap and sawdust smell.

His wife, long insane,
shuffled through the dark must of rooms
furnished in a generation of dust,
and mumbled incoherently
of a dead cousin.

The sound of his rocking—slow and sure—
troubled the old man
as did the sound of his wife's movements
and the popping of his joints
as he pushed, released.

The chores of day complete,
his wife moved to the door,
knelt there on a burlap sack
and stared silently
into the evening that enclosed them.

Silent she, silent he
rocking in the soft twilight,
until seeing some hidden sign in the moon,
each arose from his place
and walked stiffly to his bed.

        by JEANIE C. SLATTON, Purdue University, Ind.

BELLOW'S "STAG AT SHARKEY'S"

        Cigars between bared teeth,
        they sucked black air
        into their panting lungs.

        Eyes focused, intent
        they crouched forward
        on their lurking haunches.

        Their sweaty faces caught
        the tension of the punches
        thrown in the ring.

        We were drawn
        to watch the grappling stags,
        sweat dot the stretched canvas.

        Legs, arms, leather fists;
        stopped
        before the energy releasing clash.

The silent screams
in their drawn faces,
cheers roared through my senses.

The painting of an instant.
The final dimension;
I feel the force, the punches.

by D. H. FISHBURN, Case Western Reserve, Ohio

THE FREE MAN'S BURDEN

How can I stay on my own private hill
Lost in the grass with lime popsicles
Watching powderpuff clouds and my current hero
Riding by on his white stallion
While other people
Writhe on their backs in mud
Which isn't even theirs
Watching nuclear powered horseshoes
Trample them further in

by BRIAN LOBDELL, University of Idaho

THE COUNTRY

"We can afford to separate (the decadent few that
are misguiding the nation's youth) from our soci-
ety—with no more regret than we should feel over
discarding rotten apples from a barrel."

SPIRO T. AGNEW

I

The sky's made mirrors of the ground
And worships reflection graved of cloud—
Tears upon itself,
Split limbs upon straight trees,
Gray upon green:
    O torn country,
Whose clouds have spent themselves
           for themselves
Crippling the corn,
Drowning the tomatoes in seedy blood

II

Cold rain began,
Ripped ties of the land,
        to hot,
And steam raffs rise after seven days—
    A dove
Looking for footspace in its image,
And shrieking "life life" into depths of swamp
And deceased stalks into the interland;
         Steam
Beating upon a coma of the land,
And language is every water mirror

III

Fall liberates
Its leaves twist midair
To golden rot,

And storm upon the embassies of the clouds:
                    Unconditional involvement
Of the wet will not be long:
Leaves fall the power of the mirror

IV

Under the ground a spring churns,
Welling beneath a flesh of earth—
         Water
Filters time-honored through the rocks,
Leaving language behind
In sifted clumps of the country;
Under ground, water is pured in time,
O, and finds fire into the earth core:
Water waits to be tapped

V

It could have been a good faith summer—
The farmers say to their feet,
Whose shoes drown themselves in black swamp,
Whose toes hide from the intermist
                    and blood mosquitoes,
Spacevoided mist upon the very land
Into blocks of space christ and natural trash
And sunken fields of glass
                              mirror
                                impossible
                                    images,
              And spring, spring
Is a winter and white anarchy away:
And life is under ground:
And water waits to be tapped

                    by JAMES GRABILL, College of Wooster, Ohio

LATE GOTHIC
—an end for the cycle—

I.

Tiny capitals
decorate but don't disturb
the thrusting
stems of stone surging
whitely upwards
only to terminate
in the cool flatness
   of a mildly pointed arch.

II.

Eight-sided fountain
Quatrefoil panels of veiny
      marble
Glass ball lulled in the
      thrust of the water-spout.
Troubadour's hymns
On the lips and limbs of others'
      ladies
Whose high red heels
      make pedestals precarious.

III.

And Mary perched
On a pagan altar
Fondling the Baby
On her knee, not unlike
Eros and Aphrodite.

by CHARLES A. PETRY, Cleveland State University, Ohio

DANCE OF THE BLOODLETTERS

A rhythmic game completely unrestrained—
This savage outcry of body gymnastics.
Hurling movements and native chants
Burst out, wildly effortless.
The imbalance fragments the
Form into casual artlessness;
The reality of being possessed in
A life of darkness, perhaps.

The white observer strains to align
Imbalance, finds the forbidden
Entry a danger both strangely
Repulsive and attractive.
Before the lifeblood of the African
bush there were graveyards
and coffins to explore. Now,
the struggle too near the open
flames feels loose, intense.

Life that falls apart in subway stations
And dark alleyways breathes
Heavier here. Not caught ajar, or
masqueraded—but on a verge of
vitality: seductive motion
in a twilight jungle. no
immediate promise or penalty—
Only flailing, naked bodies . . .
Look of invisible invitation . . .
Fumes of burning ash and sweat.

The uselessness bids an acceptance;
Sensuality without costume
Utterly honest and natural.
A well-worn mask, perhaps,
but not really immoral enough
to cover the observer's repression—
The urge to leap within

Why this shame and embarrassment?
the edge of discovery but the
proximity of respectability.
That is the white man's reason
why the graveyards are simpler:
The gut has already been cut;
that darkness holds no superstition
For decayed flesh or the idle dead.

by M. ANNE HEINE, Grove City College, Pa.

A QUARTER CENTURY RETROSPECT

Maybe someday a young girl
Will throw my poem down in disgust;
Thinking that such sensitivity
Is extravagantly vulgar
against the steel structure
that has become her body.

An endless influx of music, men,
aestheticism and flower to help
scoop out the chasm that divides
             THE VACUUM.

And so a poem fills an hour
that divides day from night.
Some people ease the light's
transition from their souls in
             OTHER WAYS—
but who cares if spring comes again anyway!
Three passed through me . . . where's
The netting torn?
What is the thread composed of
        that can help me mend?

by PAULA STONE, Wayne State University, Mich.

137

AN EASTER ELEGY, 1965, BEFORE
AND AFTER

On a Saigon hill
the calendar is flapping still
while women step lightly with lily
click
click
click
east of Central Park.
Below, the subway
BEHOLD A GREAT EARTHQUAKE
and the guards in Saigon shake
and the Potomac Pentangle trembles.
Helicopters cluck above Fifth Avenue
shooting white virgins
click
click
click.
HIS APPEARANCE IS LIKE LIGHTNING
Saigon cunt love Jesus
no fuck Friday,
Easter free.
Green fronds flourish round fecund bomb ponds in Haiphong
DC cherry children search for colored eggs on White House
    Lawn.
WHY DO YOU SEEK THE LIVING
In presidential pockets boxes stencilled
"THIS SIDE UP"
"HEAD"
Happy Easter:
I wait for you in Saigon soil—
Dig, children, dig beneath the pink and red air
dig, but he won't be there
because bay-bee he are on are-and-are
gone; a vacate, a lack he are.
Meanwhile, parade charades the Avenue into
a wave gay by Patrick's waxy Pope
Welcome Jesus, Sir, and blessed be all rabbits today.

Menwhile, VC burrow into subway tubes
creating
premature rush hours
and send messages to all the world that
tick
tick
tick
all the good people are in the arms of Jesus
and that New York is a free fire zone.
Tell the rest in lotus petals as they fall
Tell the story ever after all
Cheer the chorus
tenor toll in the picture tower of teevee
tick
tick
tick.
Yet I wait for you
till the calendar be still
and silence tell the rising time, when
SUPPOSING HIM TO BE THE GARDENER
the lost HEAD man
that all-risen man
raise him again,
raise them all;
come back,
roll back the rocks,
come back . . .
click
click
click,
tick
tick
tick. . . .

by GEORGE SEBOUHIAN, Ohio State University

MEMORIAL DAY SCENE:
Commemorating the Dead

there is a traffic jam in the graveyard Pontiacs and Fords
bumping around in the stones ladies with lace hats and men
with shining black shoes trail through the dust the sun
raises heat waves from their shadows which move along at
twice the speed of light everyone is staying too long
the parking meters are running out of time and a street
walker with a badge is giving out special tickets
for the holidays sick from the smell of flowers children
are playing in a fresh dug grave two lovers are making it
on the spot of Smith dogs are digging in the close clipped
grass around the feet of the omens from the suburbs they
have all worn their special masks for the festival

the cars are at a standstill as the gates begin to close
a young lady begins to play a flute a single moan joins it
and soon everyone is joining in for harmony the wails
syncopate chanted from breath to breath creating a warm fog
enveloping the whole area the people begin to disintegrate
evaporate from sight from formlessness the old ones rise up
out of the earth brushing off the penicillin hairs and
the dust of their leisure moving and dancing away the fog
clears they are all getting into the cars a governor is
directing traffic and the new faces go away like turned sod

by MICHAEL HAYS, University of Illinois

ON A CASTRATION

Blazing meteors in the Artic's chilling whiteness,
Bolingbroke's madness,
Iago's silence,
A young woman's wet fire
Recalled by an extinguished man;
These—these all are unnatural.

140

Spent wood should be let
To forget the sapling;
Forgetting is not forsaking.
And Abelard's memory,
In equanimity,
Should have been severed too.

by KENNETH A. KOTTKA, University of Oklahoma

ELEGY

Sheep scatter all over
In the meadows now.
If the troll at the bridge
Does not snatch them,
They manage to slip
From the sides of the bridge.
Yes, their wool weights
    them down;
No-one will stop the drownings
Because Bo-Peep was abducted
And some sneaky dog
From another fairy tale
Made off with her staff
As a joke on the sheep
And on Moses and on
The twenty-third psalm.

by MARILYN BLITZSTEIN, Kent State University, Ohio

SHOREFOLK

Now idle his leads lie tangled,
His spoons of a sharded crust,
His trots a fisted snarling and
His reels are gone to rust,
His seines to dust;
His rods lie webbed, his boathouse
Cocked upon crazy legs
With its pier lapped out to tongue the tide
That rimes with its dregs;
Where green secrets stow their eggs,
Washes low; its wave-run planks
By seasons scored,
And by evening never a gull goes
By its gilling board;
Time was they by sevens soared;
Time was dawn saw him
Moon-waning or moon-shine,
A silver man in silver sedge set
Against sable pine,
Setting a silver line;
Silver in time's beholding tide-run
And evening eye,
Spring and fall in a wind
He offered a silver fly
To the runing river by;
There in the runed running
By rifting winds he found
Riddles, fingered ruins
Of ancient shorefolk drowned;
Time was they throve and towned
By waters, waded,
Wooed and wived their kind,
And rove their sons in a patterned running,
Wide-mouthed and reed-ribbed lined,
Boned like fish, and chined;
There among wastings
Winnowed a fisher-man's child,

Sun of his summers, a season's reigning
By water; ways beguiled
Him, the river wild;
There among wastings
Luck in his hand lined, knurled
Him red catches (shouldering beaches,
Lapped shallows pooling, purled)
And gaffing his youth was, girled;
There among wastings
Aged; time began
Backwards, the wash of water, winter-fed
Roiled as the spring, and the lines ran
Red; for the fisher-man
There among wastings
He rove him a singular weight
He cast, and the water, the winds back-lashed,
And his fisher's-boy bled for bait
And the red ran; a ramming rate
There among wastings
Of gulls didoed like girls, dove
To the shallows smacking, a frenzy of fish!
Crack! his heart divided, rove,
Ran out in red; red love
There among wastings
Breeches, deep and running sounds,
Salt blood of the fisher-man's gilly children!
In a watered pocket confounds;
His mouth a red wound
There among wastings
He cursed! and the line and the trebled hook
Yawed, and the water yawned apart,
Read like any book,
And the fisher-man shrank to look
There among wastings,
But ran to high ground;
Hauled in, the gulls for birdy reasons
Rolled like pigeons, the tide turned round,
The wood ran a circle of seasons,
The first man drowned;

143

There among wastings
He has found him a cove to ride in
And has worked him a harp,
A silver spoon for the plucking
Cunning runs he cast once; rolls
Him old songs, and the scrolls
Are the heads of sucking carp
Among wastings
He rolls, and a runic grin
At the cud of time is his cut mouth,
Kelped at his ankle, his shivered shin,
And rolls as the tide in
Among wastings
Carols what glad songs? these of the swan-road
Ride: Titanic dives in the eye of the sun's
Aye, by God since the first green surges
Crabbed those cunning oars, deaths begun,
Drowned man and fisher-man, one
Among wastings
To the watered day
He sings good luck to the killing water,
Fisher-men's sons, good luck to their blondest daughter,
Spawning in rapids, the rivers raping,
Their ancient lays
Hipped in red, at the world's last cape
They cast in the Milky Way.

by THOMAS R. THORNBURG, Ball State University, Ind.

WINTER IN SCANDINAVIA

If you weren't so far away
I'd kiss you.
But since you're where you are,
I guess my pillowcase will have to do.

I remember a time once, in Sweden,
when I was as lonely as I am now.

A courtyard,
if you could call it that,
except that courtyards are green,
and whisper of warm times;
Not of cold, and snow,
and dirty windows frozen shut
on a fifteen Kronor room.

2

The snow has stopped now.
There are a few people on the street below,
Though the cold still hurts.

It's only four blocks to the restaurant on MasterSamuelsgatan,
where they have the greasy, sweet smelling sausages called Korv.
Only five to the new place with the English menus,
and "Three Crown" beer.

I'd go there and have some more Swedish spaghetti
if there was someone there I could talk to,
And if it wasn't so damned cold outside.

3

I'll probably end up hungry,
helping the desk clerk with his "English" again.
If it was only a little warmer
I think I'd go to the railroad station,
and buy my ticket to Oslo.

by TIM WOODWARD, University of Idaho

HEY BROTHER!

Hey, brother,
where do you pitch your tent?

In the black chicken-run
you call the brood of your madness
and rear them.

Your cock's trumpet
crows wounds into the air—

You have fallen from the nest
like a naked bird
passers-by eye
that brazenness.

True to your native land
you sweep the roaring meteors
back and forth with a nightmare broom
before the flaming gates of Paradise . . .

Dynamite of Impatience
pushes you out to dance
on the tilted flashes of inspiration.

Your body gapes points of view
you recover the lost
dimensions of the pyramids
with a mindful eye
     and
a sun-lit soul

Birds
sitting in the branches of your eye
twitter to you the blossoming geometry
of a map of stars.

Night unfolds
a chrysalis of enigmatic moss
in your Budweiser hand

until you hold the wing-breathing butterfly of morning
quivering—
quivering—
with a soulful cry
you drink its blood.

by DUANE R. CLARK, Wisconsin State University

REQUIEM FOR NATURE

Land of wind and trees,
the sycophant has come
sacrificing the beauty of motherhood
for the wealth of the assassinated earth.

Sleep a deep death.
Your resurrection will
be the end of man,
for he is your only killer,
blind to the manifest daylight
ignorant of the shadow's beauty.
"Forgive them Father, for
they know not what they do."

In knowledge as it is in ignorance,
In sight as it is in blindness,
In sanity as it is in madness,
In life as it is in death.

Sleep a deep death.
Your resurrection will be the
end of man,
for he is your only killer.

by JAMES A. KELLNER, Kent State University, O.

LADY OF THE DREAM

In dreams the three eyed lady
with raven locks and gleaming sword
is nothing strange to me
I meet her at the end of long dim halls
Or dancing furiously on shining floors
And wish she would tell me something more . . .

For knowledge glitters in all her eyes
her lips form a cruelly mocking smile
Yet when I wake with her image
still tingling in my eyes
I realize she has told me nothing, nothing at all.

by CAROLE LEVIN, Southern Illinois University

A FLAME EXTINGUISHED

I.

Passing stranger! Do you not know how longingly I look upon
 you,
You must be he I was seeking. . . .

   Sunrise and a swelling breeze
   Frost blue transparence off Hyannis,
   Tugging skiffs against their moorings,
   Stirring gulls nestled in shallows,
   Shaking sleep from solemn pines.

   Breeze of summer, cooled with mist,
   Sprays rippling sand, bejeweling the sky,
   Refracting a single brilliance
   Into countless gems descending
   To tousled hair of boys, pausing
   To scan the flashing bay for scudding sails.

148

II.

The force that through the green fuse drives the flower
Drives my green age. . . .

In a time when defoliated trees revealed a war,
When paunchy uniforms sported big cigars,
When the ill-hinged door to a frontier
Where every voice was not packed in crumpled newspaper
And boxed off into attics, creaked shut,
Thousands shook their heads and turned away,
Bearing silent hopes in private arks.
Those seeking the wilderness, those thousands,
Craned their necks to devour vital words,
Drank of miraculous, sparkling wine,
And would not silence one able
To string the stiffened bow,
Launching words for vague frustrations,
One to bear a new-cut lance upright
In staled winds of stagnant commands.

III.

Season of mists and mellow fruitfulness

Strolling solitary on a desert beach in Oregon,
Through the surf, through the cooling waves
Splashing his bared ankles and turned-up cuffs,
Avoiding burning—sometimes shifting—sand,
He balances against the undertow
Like a tightrope walker, eyes intent,
Despite sand and wind ruffling his hair,
Despite sun's glare, hardening his face
Into a plaster mask, never losing
The juncture of shore and cloudless sky.

IV.

It is a sea of faces about them in agony, in despair

until the horror of the race dawns staggering the mind,
the whole sea becomes an entanglement of watery bodies
lost to the world bearing what they cannot hold.

> Descent from sun-scorched podium
> Into no-man's land of outstretched hands
> Clutching, sucking him into the whirlpool
> Swirling up from Newark and Washington,
> Brushing, as a whore's hair in the night,
> Across Appalachia and Navajo country.
> Desperate eyes demand him whose name
> Their bodies bear, crying for help.
> He grasps them, skin to skin, probing
> Beneath their sun-baked shells for living meat.

V.

Then Sir Bedivere cried and said, "Ah, my lord Arthur,
what shall become of me, now ye go from me and leave
me here alone among mine enemies?"

A roaring waterfall of victory cannot silence
Pistol bursts, staccato rimshots to end a march.
Instead of hopes, the dying brain
Harbors dulled, leaden slugs.
Sprawling bodies and splattered blood clog
The hallway from the nation to the victory room.
The great cloud darkens the morning-muffled world:
Glints of ignorance expire with spreading news—
Embers no longer comforting—and dimness is all.

VI.

O strong dead-march you please me!
O moon immense with your silvery face you soothe me!
O my soldiers twain! O my veterans passing to burial!

Sorrow seeps, then swirls, from California
To the East, enflamed into a comet,
Winding, carrying New York's heart to Washington.
All under a dark, bulging, stifling cloud,
Overpregnant, lined with blood.
Saturday: week's end, evening:
Torchlight marks sloping curves to the hilltop,
Silent with milling people, with nothing to clutch,
Hands jammed into hiding, weeping.

VII.

My brothers—both had ceased to breathe. . . .

I am to wait . . .
I am to see that I do not lose you.

Leaden evening

Upon concrete canyoned mirrors,
Littered with posters and shattered glass,
Blankets the young
Stunned on a whore's vermined bed.

Whipping red and white
Light a man bending to free
A sword charred among the rubble
Of a blasted cathedral.

                    by JAY S. PAUL, Michigan State University

IN RIDDLED FAITH

(for GPS)

Once I was afraid to travel in the dark,
Like the thief shuddering on his cross
Praying softly in stringed curses.
Laughing in a crowd,
I knew I was lonely, . . . and bored.

A stranger beckoned me to follow him,
I walked beside him with light-filled eyes
    on stumbling feet.
He brought me books and songs on silver,
Taught me to throw stones, . . . and flowers.
He kissed me with his freedom.

Kneeling wide-eyed in a bare room:
    "This strange guide will be destroyed,
    It must be my hand."
I dressed myself in a suit of flowers
And marched to meet him in the meadows.

His blood spilled warm and bright
Over my sweating, trembling hands.
I denied his three screams three times.
The blood stone lay at his feet,
Tears washed his still cold face.

My reeling senses danced to a stop.
Mary Mother of God, I've taken My life!
Yet I'm burning!
Now I trip unafraid through the empty darkness,
Armed only with clear, fingerprint memories.

    by MARILYN KAY ADAMS, Central Michigan University

IMAGE TO EZEKIEL

Look to the hills of the north,
for within their chambers of imagery
fathers now eat sour grapes
and set their children's teeth on edge,
and draw swords.

The scum is not lifted from the boiling pot
nor the grass covered with dust
to become a place for nets, yet
she plays the harlot, naked,
the flaw of the shards.

A conspiracy of prophets, and now
rich Tyrus moves to the pit,
the tree cut down in its aging spring,
branches shuddering, yet
no one hears the child's cry
echoed in the street,
and the muted horn declares unequal judgment
as Egypt burns.

Only a valley of bones
and someone to place a sign for burial,
for the pit has reality
and the question of equality
lies in dust, unanswered,
no bare place to green.

For who listens in bare land
but hears the echo of horns and blood,
battle crys and altar bait,
where offerings become offers
and how much depends upon addition.

by JAMES REIGEL, University of Wisconsin

THE GHOST OF KEATS

He can no more hope the uninked page to
   Throb echo-polished than again to clench
   The baby-rightful bosom of some wench,
Or cheat Time's changeful-hidden rendezvous
   Whatever it be for you: Whether it
Be to learn crooked landscapes where men gaze
On nothing through a battle-noisy haze,
   Or to some cottage-eager lass submit.

I cannot sketch those blazon-faded skies
   For you here on my chatter-gilded sheet,
His angel-whispers, or his mournful sighs
   So bingo-nervous to at magic slave
   Await their song that never will seem sweet
Enough, and a small, blossom-stinking grave.

by WILLIAM CHALEK, Northeast Missouri State

WHEN I WAS OUTSPOKENLY YOUNG

When I was outspokenly young,
My father and I would journey
Through Van Cortlandt Park,
Down by the sonorous Hudson.
Life was a sweet tooth then,
My pockets about to burst,
Stuffed with enough nougat
To munch the wonderous hours.
Around the dangerous crags
We would watch the old men sniggle,
Jerking monstrous eels ashore.

Such arduous routine astounded me;
And I jumped upon a rough rise,
Shouting, I wanna be an eel-catcher!
Pouting, I wanna be an eel-catcher.

But the yells of eels were louder,
Much louder than a mouthful of goo.

by GEORGE M. FLYNN, Campbellsville College, Ky.

A CHANGE—OF COURSE

and my fingers no longer trail gently
through the quiet, bubbling wake
of a slowly drifting boat,
and my eyes are not turned toward the sky
watching the soft rounded mounds of water
disguise themselves as good weather,
and I no longer smile
at the caprice in your playful hands
nor the fire flashing
in your eyes
(pretending to be burning)
and as you fall
from my rigid thoughts,
even then! yes,
even then,
I will not look behind your gaze
sorrowful as I may find it,
for I have found you a selfish
ever constant bowsman,
and though the waters trailed gently
in the beginning,
they are lashing and twisting
and spinning in the harbour,
the stern forgotten

155

as you speed toward madness,
the sky ignored, though it says, "good weather,"
and watch! my obsessed bowsman,
or can you see?
the blood from my fingers, caught
in the rudder,
the blood from my fingers, churning
in the water;
look again! and you will see
mutiny on your vessel,
look again, and you will see
I have chosen the waters . . .
at least we equally
displace each other.

by JO LAWSON, Rockford College, Ill.

When John the Human Cannon Ball
Defined the horizons
With his comet's tail,
And the Earth spun and sparkled
And burned with red, white, and blue fire,
We held our head high
And pointed our phallic pistol
At the womb of the world.
Power was to our finger
As warm honey in our hair,
And we trod on the writhing masses with our
Silver spangled boot.
And God looked on with a frown.
But from the corners of his frown
We hung pinyatas,
And we tickled his ribs
And chewed his fingers.
And Selma, the soft white goddess
Spread her thighs,

And we built a fifteen lane highway
Into her womb,
And hung a big green sign over it that read
In big white letters
BRING ME YOUR POOR, YOUR SICK, YOUR HUNGRY.
And the neon eye
At the center of the universe
Blinking eternally
Silently shed an electric tear,
While Sphinx chewed bodies,
And burped an arm, or a leg,
Having forgotten her question.

by STEVE MASON, Adrian College, Mich.

TO MY MOTHER

I remember her now as she was
when I was younger,
when she sat, tired as old glass,
with a book in her lap, and
no page turned for an hour.

I remember her on circled days
singing dusty Lutheran hymns in Finn,
laughing when we all forgot the words.

I remember her flannel nightgown,
and her on the floor
over an endless round of solitaire
when one of us was late.

I remember her pausing in mid-life
to change her sex;
her worried tears and fears, not knowing
that this difference made no difference,
that in our innocence we
could not care enough.

by D. PHILLIP BURNSIDE, Illinois Wesleyan University

SANDRA

Dawn in plush and silent roar
  Booming, crushing lonely blooming
    Sandra—pearl of seagreen sadly
   Warbling hawthorn war-thrush fluting
Dawn in plush and silent roar

   Spiked and jingling cold tympanum
  Morning's breaking hardly dying
Sandra—pearl of seafoam sighing
  Cracked and bleeding bright stars fading
   Dawn in plush and silent roar

Dusty steel and golden hoofbeats
  Beating, pounding loudly booming
   Sandra—pearl of heart-hung satin
  Lis'ning for the velvet's dawning
Dawn in plush and silent roar

by **BILL DOWNY**, University of Idaho

Sitting high above highway 119
pine-cones at my feet
small butterfly walks on
lichen-covered rock.
Distant slopes are blue-green
with pine-trees & haze as
dark afternoon clouds come
over the mountains.
My head dizzy, I look back down
to the stream imbedded in
the craggy canyon.

by **TERRY OLIVE**, Millikin University, Colo.

The light
filtering
through the leaves
Creates a
dappled pattern
on the grass.
The wind
moves through
the leaves
of our
tree-vaulted world
Setting
the pattern in
motion.
Flickering on
our faces,
Light and shadow
dance.

by KATHY LEE MARTIN, Franklin College of Indiana

THE AWAKENING

We gallopped
Through
A sagebrush sea
That day,
Before the pouting clouds
Swallowed the sun
And,
With wet distended lips,
Disgorged their disgust
Upon
The warm-baked earth
Beneath.

We spurred the horses—
Yours bone-black,
Mine sinewy red—
And rode
To escape the conspiracy
Howling down
Upon us.

The ice
Of a thousand
Brittle fingers
Crept
Glacier-like
Down my spine
And
Your face
Cried
A torrent of tears.

There was no place to go
        But the cabin on the hill . . .
We shivered
Sprinkling tiny cloud flecks
Upon
The pinewood floor.
There was no wood
For the fireplace
But
There was liquid fire
In your eyes
And
Gentleness,
As your touch
Pried the frozen Skeletal fingers
From my heart.

And the blackness above us
Rumbled in wrath
At the final defeat
Of its frigid messenger.

                    by JEAN NUTILE, University of Idaho
                    160

PASSING BY

On the corner as you pass the chestnut-man
Selling golden glowing sweetness,
You see his treasures go to strangers' pockets.
And not a word exchanged . . .

Then pass by flower-laden stands,
Where women pass a busy day
Brightening everyday worlds.
And never being thanked . . .

Passing by a stranger in the street,
You think of all in life that passes by.
Perhaps the stranger wonders, too,
But please don't ever ask . . .

by CATHLIN FLEMING, Mundelein College, Ill.

THE EVENING WE SPENT AT 39th
AND WILLIS

At the moment of submission,
that time when twilight
cried against the gun barrel pushed over her face;
at the moment when soldiers on leave
climb out of their insignia
to snare women in bars and the whores like
store manequins
fall on them as senseless mutterings;
at that aftertaste moment when coffee
still stretches on your tongue and
the weight of your paycheck shouts in your pocket
like a battle victor. Then,
at that instant of dying buildings,

161

you came, wearing the same face,
and a scar opened inside me and began to bleed;
the nightclub,
scotch and water and a band from the Bronx,
trite poems thudded against the walls of my mouth,
my watch pushed spears into my wrist,
the room, like a trench, enclosed me in bullets.
I cannot remember what you said,
though your finger drew circles on the rim of the glass

by GAIL TREBBE, Stephens College, Mo.

CONTINUUM

A phenomenal procession of events
   graced infinite pages of history.
The accounts mentioned
      primitive battle,
            then sophisticated warfare.
      Masquerade morality,
            then unchecked desire.
      Raw hatred,
            then distorted passion.

An observer noted his sightings:
            Progress.

by R. STEVEN GRAVES, Otterbein College, O.

162

IN NIGHT ON THE BEACH

And I and another stayed on the beach by the moon,
stealing dreams and trading pleasures and
riding stampeding stallions across the crests.

The night heaved and howled as a savage dog,
for it was the distant stranger, the silent observer,
the impotent host to the ecstatic creation of fantasy and order.

And then the sun crashed our party,
and we had to run home,
running white, naked, lustless,
sunless, and estranged.

by B. D. WRIGHT, Ball State University, Ind.

OHIO

Waters reached round the bend of trees
    boats were afloat
      one drifting
        waiting for a nibble
      the other
        making ripples as it headed for the surfing front.

fish capered occasionally
    coming up for air perhaps
    or protesting against men who invade their haven
        causing ripples on the placid expanse
a black widow fell from above
  on the butterfly perched my my knee.

many creatures dwell here
    permanently, I guess
but they made room for me to sit among them.

163

from this vantage point
            I can view nature from the massive rocks at the river's bend
            and joy in the Ohio's bigness and calmness
                        except for the river barge.

by SISTER M. BENEDICTA CLAUSS, OSB,
St. Benedict College, Ind.

MOLLY

always slipping through . . .

I

The lock from Craig's Hardware
never keeps my treehouse door shut
and Molly always slips through
to have me walk her down
to Willey's Drug
where she spends her pennies
on the candies with the colors she likes
while I stand behind the sundries counter
and finger a bottle of something
too big to fit into my pocket

and then I slip down on my knees
and crawl to the magazine counter
to flip through the women books
and find the one Billy talked about all day
with everything showing

Molly goes on
with a penny's worth of this
and a nickel's worth of that
and she asks me over the counter
if I have a nickel
because she's a little short

164

and Wiley will take away
her jawbreakers
if I don't give her nickel
But what could I say
with my eyes all full
of Billy's woman

II

That first strange time
with things all tight and hard
and my wondering where it had come from

Mom noticed my spotted underwear
and the old man
heard my bouncing bed springs

In the mornings before breakfast
I'd wake up all at attention
and wondering what Molly was like
without her new summer dress
and sometimes I'd dream of a woman
from Willey's girly stand
and wake up with things
all tight and hard
only to hear the morning papers
hitting the screen door

But then my oily skin disappeared
and Billy and I laughed
at our schoolboy embarrassment
over a swollen fly
and how we'd walk with our hands in our pockets
to keep the girls from seeing
and how we'd search through Wiley's counters
to find a protection
against Billy's middle-aged whore
he'd found living
down behind Jason's Garage.

165

But I remember the park
where Mrs. Williams caught me fondling Molly
and the railway shack where I hid for hours
and the axle grease I sat in
and had to explain to Mom

I thought I'd run away
and become a hobo
or maybe a general in the foreign legion
But Mrs. Williams forgave me
and kept Molly in her daughtered eyes
while I drank Sally's lemonade
and hid behind her mother's
high backed couch

Molly woke me in my dreams
but Janie packed her baskets
for picnics down by Odom River
where she swam with just
a string of dime-store pearls around her neck

But always Molly
pulling up her dress
in my dreams

III

Saturdays and the auction
with Molly taking the buyer's receipts
and my prodding the bulls
and horses
up the loading ramps
and into the trucks

Molly's old man yodels out the figures
and catches the hands
of the farmers
as they take the bids
with a chew of tobacco
high in their cheeks

At noon
there's a basket of chicken
and a mason jar of cool water
to share with Molly
in the bed of her old man's truck
with its canvas top
keeping away the sun
and the eyes of the old men
sitting on the benches
outside the auction barn
and talking over the prize bulls
they'd seen come and go

by GREGORY CANTRELL, Southern Michigan University

BONDS

When children glue and bind and paste and tape,
Like birds that build and fashion with such cares,
Constructing shapes as Vulcan's faithful heirs,
They understand how objects take their shape;
But should the bond go deeper, men escape,
As rabbits struggling loose from hunters' snares,
Or priests involved in nothing else but prayers,
So lasting ties make mankind stand agape.
For once created, bonds are truly free
To bind the soul with lack of hate and scorn,
If men are wont to love in great degree,
Else bonds are futile, men are left to mourn,
And loss of love like raging swirling sea,
Will drown the soul that first for love was born.

by FRATER TOM GROSS, O.S.C.,
St. Francis College, Ind.

THE CREEK

Down the hill,
    behind the barn
    and past the pond,
the creek lies tangled
    in the willow grove.
Like an S upon S,
    it slithers, slips and swirls
    from the coming-in-place
    to God-knows-where:
The Atlantic Ocean, maybe,
or the Mississip',
    or Tom Glenn's dammed-up lake.
I don't know where it goes;
    I don't really care.
Right now it's making
    an S of itself.

by **DIANA NEWQUIST, Northeast Missouri State Teachers College**

IN THE WELFARE ROOM

Black Mrs. Bonaparte,
her large loose breasts
sprawled beneath a faded
two-buck cotton print,
her listless tired eyes,
bloodshot, staring blankly
into the noon-game nothingness
every other midday
in the welfare room,
asks through rotten yellow-stained
tobacco teeth
for shoe money.

Black Mrs. Bonaparte
in less than forty years
of counting days by mouthfuls,
counting work by white man floors
they let her scrub,
and nights by whiskey studs
she took when good Willie went bad
some fifteen years back,
calls eleven kids her own,
and asks the clean white face
for shoe money.

Black Mrs. Bonaparte
a particle of flesh grown huge
in Harlem,
lost number twelve to rats,
saw number six Elmo
lose a leg to a drunk-driven Cadillac
on the play street,
watched number two Dinah
writhe on the kitchen floor
and spit out Wilma,
fruit of the rape
in the school back-stairwell,
and buried once good Willie
with the three cop bullets self-defense
chest high and in the groin.

Black Mrs. Bonaparte
will settle for shoe money,
and wander out to
find another filthy white man john
to scrub. Black Mrs. Bonaparte sweats, oozing
water from every dark skin fold,
and feels the summer coming on.
Yes, the hot summer trouble, Lord,
fires, cops, shooting,
like when number one Vince
was gone with little Bill for three long nights.

by IRA SHOR, University of Wisconsin

169

REALITY

It was early when I started out
now my makeup is old, my lips cigarette swollen,
and my thoughts simply circular.
I see you clearly tonight but it isn't enough
I am jealous of the necessary thoughts that keep me
from thinking about you.
Things get worse with the smoke and the beer:
the clearness of you fades.
I want to write about you to keep you constant
but my pen is frozen
and the smell of smokey joes is getting to me.

Tomorrow is here and I am a thousand miles from your dawn
facing one more day thinking of how it is without you.

by JANE S. FURLONG, St. Benedict College, Ind.

Rudufus, sleeping under a tree
opposite the profane domain
of a narcotic bee.

While, the fan in the window spun
a blurry slimy silvery glow
that chopped up the bee's widow.

The bee, off his usual path
stung the man in the mouth
a decision made during bath.

Rudufus, gave a rueful laugh
as his jaw dropped
and the fan stopped.

by BRUCE SANDERSON, Stout State University, Wis.

AN OVERTURE

Poet and Peasant
            music that mingled at first
life vapors perfuming the air.
      NOTES
   opening up and speaking
of a perplexed, prophetical
                  GIANT
—squeezed—
   into a thimble
                  of misunderstandings
                  of wornout cliches
                  of doorslamming damnable doubts
Poet and Peasant
            music that mingled at first
      then reverberated loudly, wildly
Poet and Peasant
            then rejected itself
            before the refrain.

by M. J. DE DOLPH, Marquette University, Wis.

FIRST MILD DAY IN MARCH

When web strung eyes
peer from caves and ground
to see where from
the diamond water sounds come,
blood and senses stretch
to join the harmony.

This being that time of year
my muscles and mind, jingling
with all that stirs about them,
are keen with remembrances of Springs before.

171

They recall the sounds, sighs,
and the taste of smiles—
    they've known them all.
Yet, there is an innocence
in each Spring not spoiled
by experience. Knowledge
is the enzyme of anticipation

as this time of year
rises green
from white ashes.

by DAVID HOLZAPFEL, Marietta College, O.

LAUGHTER

Twinkling eyes betray booming sounds
Carrying cheer to all around

The plague is spreading far and wide
Like lapping rivulets from the tide

Beware you prophets of gloom and sorrow
Its catching, catching, catching
You'll have it on the morrow
The dread disease of laughing

by SISTER TERESA SCHNEIDER, Marillac College, Mo.

EAST AND WEST

While mighty brazen ships
Steamed forth,
Leaving wakes awash,
And gleaming in the sun;
And birds of steel wings

Screamed defiance!
Trailing plumage white
Against the blue—
While under frothy topaz seas,
Long piercing shadows
Swam the deep in earnest,
The East was dozing—
Dreaming of a pun,
To shock the West, in pretense,
That knew what had segun.
That knew what had begun.

by MILTON SCHAUT, Idaho State University

PUPPETS

grease-painted faces of no one
dance on an unwanted stage.
the puppet plays
but without laughter.
people look but do not see
for no one cares.
the puppet cries invisible tears
and sinks to himself.
wooden epitaph
of things gone.

by JOHN F. NEAL, Briar Cliff College, Ia.

SINGLE

So like a morning
      without sun
    drenched in a damp
       covered mantle
          of cluttering noises

—Fearful—
lest someone peel
it all away
lest there be silence
and no one there
—no one but
me alone.

Gently,
half-willingly
stripped—
I stand dismantled
waiting—
in the dark
in the cool jet blackness
trusting—
So like a morning
without sun
drenched in a damp
covered mantle
of silence
—Expectant—

by SR. DOLORES KUEFFLER, Marillac College, Mo.

AUTUMN LEAVES AND WET GRASS

You know how it is with autumn leaves and wet grass,
How their fragrance overwhelms the senses.
—When October brings "fall" and "winter" together in a dance,
And you dance along with them, among the leaves;
not caring about wet shoes;
And each step is joy, and each leaf stirred, a memory.

by EDWARD DELONAS, Idaho State University

DIVINA COMMEDIA

A bloody bird cringes lofty
towards the lapsing sun.
Crimson droppings mark
his way on earth.
His wings trim
like desert heat.
He moans his last sound
        He is an alabaster trailing moss
        like a Medusa
to the unknowing.
He squeals a stuck thought
        Chained Prometheus
        flailing his limbs
to the gods.
If he turns
to fly into the wind
it is over, in a feathered explosion.
With mercy
        To the natural
he will flee for the sun
and fall,
to be buried in the cooling sod.

        by JAMES R. WEBER, St. Olaf College, Minn.

STRAWBERRY SEASON

In strawberry season,
when all eyes are raised
to discover anew the sky,
and tomorrow is something west,
awaiting the sun,

The whistling milk man
peeks over a fence
to bark at a dog.

by JOSEPH A. VANDEKIEFT, Henry Ford
Community College, Mich.

WHEN IN SEASON

(with Dedication to J.G.)

When in season the leaf-fall is bright on earthen paths,
The stone walks are crystalled with white,

Colors are strewn on velvet greens,
When the solid liquid falls away,
    like a screen hiding a canvas beneath.
From the south, small tinged birds whisk
    in newly leafed trees, designing a
    nest for pigmented boughs.

When in season, great stalks of yellow
    kernels fill the fields
    of earth, while wild plants
    desperately seek a high place to climb.

A sea of chaff coated golden wealth sways
    with the brush of a breeze,
Spreading a sun smear above the richly
    browned ground.

When in season, as the red orange ball
    moves to the edge of a
    waterless blue sea, the nut,
    apple, kernel and leaf begin to fall.
The dark and aged furrows are reaped
    and the climbers fall away.

Little nests, of bird, long abandoned,
and that of the mouse, its strength renewed,
when in the corner of a wood a burrow is made more
secure.

And after a minute, in the stroke
of a black angry cloud,
The hills, valleys and darkened
limbs are covered again in a pure
crystalline snow.

by MICHAEL WHITMAN, St. Meinrad College, Mich.

THE CELESTIAL TINKER

the golden-maned lion stalks through the tall trees
to the plateau
to the height overlooking the quiet valley

sundrops of flowers spot the field
and the breeze bends with music coming
strumming from the lute of the long dark man
who squats
atop a flat grey table of stone.

tinker-man making a song—
shaping it of the sun.
he sings. the song comes. it is a prayer.
and the sun and the prayer become one
in the songs that the tinker-man hums.

in the forest the golden-maned lion
moves with the shake of his golden limbs.

by SUZANNE MARIE BUCKLEY,
Case Western Reserve, Ohio

LOST

I walk in silent dreams through blurred illusions
of distorted figures silhouetted against a blood-red sky.

I can't hear music
or laughter
as do the foolish philosophers.

I hear the wail of a poor baby, and the insane buzzing
of flies over plump, greasy garbage cans.

The sun is hot and torments my aching shoulders.

A sudden flash of hope sparks somewhere in the
back of my mind, and I desperately try to grasp it.
It fades, and I am grieved.

A teasing shadow of a once beautiful thought
creeps into my memory, but fleets away before my
hungry mind can savor it.

I am numb once more.

A flashing light warns "Don't Walk, Don't Walk."
I walk on.

by ELAINE AMBROSE, University of Idaho

I, NOW IN MY ADAM'S EDEN

I, now in my Adam's Eden, where once heaped
Clay shaped the way around my first boy fallen
Hooky in the morning sun-rising, and together
Blaspheming labors to prospect the fruit laden
Planet. A Sabbath sunned couching about

The Garden horizon of my youth; forever leaping
        Dawns of halo showers, seeding jonquils telling
   Shoulder to wrist, blooming sheepishly, to gather
Homestead land of new found fields, widening
   Around the early sun, pushing my Adam out.

I, now in my Adam's labor, upon the birthstone
        Earth the sunlight midwife brought forth breath
   In my dust from the blood-flecked soil and where
From my Adam's rib split chest sprang Eden;
   Complete in his flesh standing before creation.
The milky Way paths lead down the Eden wood in
        Steps toward my Adam's head and heart, where death
   Waves youth above Paradise and aged fears
Pluck away upon the fruit fields always leading
   My Adam's hand in rays of eternal elation.

I, now in my Adam's Orchard, multiplying the
        Subdued earth, forbidden to the universe of longing;
   I wronged the twisted serpent that speaks from
The forks of boughs, and tempts my bewildered
   Adam with nibbles of evil swollen with life.
For I am in my Orchard now, in the appled sea
        Of my Adam's heart pendulum that is swinging
   Toward the river again, then set into motion comes
The banished boy of Eden unwinding forever
   From the Ancient river lying in the clay of belief.

          by JONATHAN STULL, Upper Iowa College

      The air breaks
      as I hear the Furies
      rush screaming from their dens
      and feel their snake hair
      whip across my cheek.

The pillars of Hades
shudder beneath my body
and the dead groan
as they are awakened
from their eternal sleep.

Suddenly,
        All is silent
and I raise my eyes
in time to see
the last smoke rise
from the leveled cities.

The reflection has disappeared
along with my lizard companion
and I am alone
with a sky so lucid
that it reflects my face
and the empty plains that encircle me.

by LESLIE BAIRD, Stephens College, Mo.

POEM IN THREE PARTS

The Salvation Business

Nine abandoned crutches lean together in a wine barrel:
      "Property of
Salvation Army—75¢ Each—No Refund—No Return."

    A valley of crutches in the moonlight at Lourdes
    Or sawdust and the Faith-healer's dare,
    Gilded serpents reply
            for the nine who will die
    While carried from bed to wheelchair.

The Boss Is Also A Poet

A clerk makes room to the left of the barrel for the display of
second-hand birdcages. ("The boss wants everything alpha-
          betical.")

> Crippled old ladies and gents
> Shuffle in dark-flowered rooms,
> Those who dream through the night
>   of canaries in flight
> Wake blessing the cage and its doom.

Decoration And Prayer For The Eve Of All Saints' Day

A has-been alchemist enters with a briefcase labeled "Halloween
          Charms,
Amulets, Snakefeathers." He purchases every birdcage & crutch
     in the store.

> Limbs beyond the dark window
> Touch death with each three-fiingered leaf
> While hands by a flame
>   blossom winter-blue veins
> . . . Mascara'd for an evening of grief.

by MICHAEL J. RITZEN, University of Minnesota

IN LANGUAGE LAB

> Now—I find myself cornered by
>   cold machines.
> Enclosed by blue protectors
>   I cannot see around me.
> My ears only hear
>   the voices.
> My mind is swallowed
>   by moving sounds.

They come
     as the water over the falls
       surging until
         the force overpowers
           the rocks.

I cannot think
     for the shields have been broken,
  and now, penetrated.
Je pense à ma vie.
         Je ne pense pas.
       Je n'ai pas un tête.
        Me-trouvez,
         me-trouvez,
          vitement.

by MARCYE MANTLER, Stephens College, Mo.

ALL THOSE WHO SIT IN THIS PEW
WILL CARRY THE OFFERING

The pen has slept for what seems
A thousand sandy days filtering through
The colander dirtied with spaghetti stains.
The poet is distracted by the alcoholic heat
Released in slugged-down shot as his eyes
Water, and the dark night is poured from cruet,
Sloshing over priently fingers,
Waiting for sacrifice, using wino tears for water.

The crowded pew collected trickling sweat.
The last supper's dance began as a minuet,
Until clashing knives and forks struggled
With the breaded body, smelling of the wino's breath,
In that bell-ringing moment, the son was stripped,
And gnashing teeth gored the blood-stewed body.

by JOSEPH J. BORKOWSKI, Wayne State University, Mich.

THE EXECUTION AND THE DOMINION

Fire!
      Six riddled humans writhed on the plain.
The Genesis of it all was too trusting
      As He bequeathed "dominion
      over the fish of the sea,
      the birds of the air,
      the cattle, over all the
      wild animals and every
      creature that crawls the earth."
For it was repugnant to see the bloodglutton flies
      devouring these representatives of the dominion,
It was repulsive to know the dominion was betrayed.

Afterwards in a monument to humanity
      this remote plain of butchery
became another graft upon the conscience of mankind
      and a vulgar tatoo upon the earth
             and
The even row white stone crosses on the voiceless plain
      marked a reply to the inhuman command.

               by GEORGE J. ALLEN, University of Idaho

NURSING HOME

"Brought back to watch my beak grow
And pass the whimper mirror.
To feel the hollows fill with
What should have been artesian tears
Where careful animals watched their
Drinking place dry. And permanent staleness
Came with slowly sagging breasts.
Once padded." In whose defense?
We asked the Man.

Perhaps, the thought, it was design.
He arched his eyebrows twice in time.
Or something to do with blowing winds;
Unhappy people with troubled sins
From eyelids that slowly rose and fell.
Mistaken tide. We bid him well.

"Brought back to let a time
For lying down with someone discover . . .
  to find . . . to let time be flesh
And find its way to the wish."

by MIKE TOBUREN, Kansas State University

The long, gray days are melting
Into nights
But failing to dissolve
Flat, empty time.
Wistful, the wind whispers
More loudly
Than the ordered dimensions
Of crowded life
The forsaken past is struggling
To be forgotten,
 (Sometimes against its inner wishes)
While the future cannot promise
Good times to come.

by ALDA L. KNIGHT, Taylor University, Ind.

INTERMEZZO

A dead dandelion
Transparent in yellow wine
Downed in a dusty rug
To a drinking rhyme
Dips her mouth in a mug:

184

Dare you leave before she dances?
Dare you sing before she's sung?
Juggle your lances:
A mirrored moon has rung.

She clutches my hand
Clinging to nails of Man?
Breathing with the gasp of a tear
I whispered, and she ran
To clasp my mouth in fear.

Dare you leave before she dances?
Dare you sing before she's sung?
Juggle your lances:
A mirrored moon has rung.

by JOAN-MARY KIEL, Aquinas College, Mich.

GOING NOPLACE

(To the disillusioned Black brothers.)

Out there in front of
me are Black brothers,
who may not even know so.
Almost 200 years of
wisdom and knowledge
about what used to be,
for they can't even
see—that their world
is only as wide as the
pavement that vibrates the
echoes of Black feet
tired and weary from
walking but getting noplace.

185

Tomorrow is not
existant on Murray St.,
just yesterday and today—
sad to say its got
to be that way.
But—its not hard
to understand when
the world is only wide
as Murray St.—and the
pavement is there only
to echo the endless
vibrations of
weary Black feet.

by FREDRICK D. MITCHELL, Kentucky State College

MOONDOOM

Your filthy feet, moonmen,
have blasphemed the moon crust just
as you have spoiled the earth soil.
You have dumped the first garbage,

You of the new moon land and stand
on the dust of nothingness with
steady faith in your dustless untouchable
creator. Genesis resounds
like a bad joke off the
crusted bottoms of craters.

O moon, you must suffer
by your cycles about our planet
all the pokes prods flags Hiltons
and specious gods that will be
built upon your body.

Moondoom will be soon as man
plants missiles in seas of tranquility.
The airlines will assure
an American moon for the elite;
already the list lengthens:
a new perversion for the wealthy bored.

Over illimitable miles
we hear the men mumble praise
into the empty air.
Can they speak across the schisms
of their own cities?

by KRISTIN LEMS, University of Michigan

THE HIGHLAND LIGHT: POSTCARD AND POSTSCRIPT AT BARNEGAT

The light at Barnegat, a stapling beam
of legend, carpets a brown hulk of leg
more beautifully dark than I dare name
and timbers dry nests down through sea born fog.
It is a gibbed embrace that nails the storm
between a sailor's eye, that luffs his sail
in to a sea-sick sleep. The leg becalms
the light and spits the wind into a squall
that bursts the sea and tears the orphan's moan
into a twin that runs his ship aground.

by ROBERT J. COLLINS, Xavier University, Ohio

THE BEAT OF SILENCE

He finds each thing alive, each timeless beat
A metronome to move with, a hard heat
To light a fire with: to bend his knee and
Wait alone for the silent, graceful hand
To reassure his shoulder. Just lightly
The fingers press, as waves crumble slightly,
Peak, peak by peak, until they hold the beach
Carelessly, knowingly within their reach.
Fingers command: those fingers touch the course
Of humble plainsong sleeping at the source,
And he is free, free to bend with the beat,
His silence breaks in waves. Cleansed with the heat
Of motion, his pulses of evensong
Smooth to rest, and he embraces a long
Life, and each throb is longer life until he
Is long life, and sees the ocean in a tree.
He walks the gentle walk of sunlight,
Beginning paths to finer movement, slight,
And yet he feels like a man of essence.
He walks the silent walk and smiles silence.

by WILLIAM SCHUTTER, Hope College, Mich.

ACCEPTANCE

The cold wind in the early day, mourning
over feldspar clouds and coming down wickedly to my ruffled
        skirts,
lashes out a prophecy
and I cough blood:
Death before thirty.

I have much: many eyes and hearts cannot
perceive evening shades.
the nearly silver lavendar
of a warm day's dusk
Only alive eyes see.

And of life, I have given woman's own gift:
I have run through grass at an early age and fallen
under a shaded half-moon
above two witch trees growing
Wet wildness blossoms.

So I caution now my steadfast lily lads
to think on other dear and lesser deaths in time's lay.
importance diminishes:
rosemary means remembrance
Growing in gardens.

I must go through.

by **ROSEMARY FITHIAN, Kent State University, Ohio**

AT THE GENERAL STORE

In Bakersfield, Missouri, the town locals
gossip in the buttered light
    of a winter morning.
There is big news today. Pot-bellied
stoves cough with firewood as old men teeter
on empty orange crates, ears red with the cold.
Zeke fingers his red-checkered cap,
sucking the life from his hickory pipe.
"Dead. The Evan's boy dead."
The old men warm their wooden hands.
A silence spreads slowly
like the red glow of the stove
    diffusing the room.

Zeke wobbles his legs in front of the fire,
then barks a short dry cough.
"Heard Emil Smith's arm is a lot better."
The old men nod and clutch the image
in their eyes.
"Heard they sent the Peterson boy
to Viet Nam last week." All nod in agreement.
A fat old man stands by the window,
looking out through the grease and dirt
aged on the pane, out to the frozen
world
where snow is swept into scattered piles,
as the grain lies sterile
        on a frozen field.

        by GLEN ENLOE, Central Missouri State College

    this fellow, bob fry,

    we met him in the park
    across from our apartment

    he asked us to light
    his cigarettes his hand
    was too drunk
    and he hadn't worked for some
    while (he was a short order cook)

    bob must have told me his name
    fifty times and he shook
    my hand each time he told me
    his name

    always pulling on his mission valley
    and making me think
    that he was like my father
    must have been

        by JAMES HAINING, Quincy College, Ill.

FATE IS THE FISHER

(for Carlin Aden)

The time of gnats
was over that hot lake
where fish rose to meet and take
under the swoop of bats.

At the tethered end of Carlin's line
I listened to back lash snap
and watched for the lazy settle
but the line rose in surprise.

It was a bat,
an erratic dart
of constant escape,
that had taken. And was taken
into the living fear of warm blood.

Very brown eyes held it away
in a hand that trembled only later
at the minded voice of those other eyes.

There was no head, no mouth,
only a shaped diamond
of serrated, raw, pink throat.

I held a rubber wing
away from the beating
body. The other wing—broken—
tapped counter-point
to the pulse in my fingers.

Carlin's fingers—two—thick as bats
fumbled at the badge on the mammal's breast
where an echo in shadow placed it
and fate—that fishes with every man.

It is not the gurgle of cold blood on grass
but life which spurts hot in his hands
that puts soul in the creel of the poet
where flying fish kick through the deep break.

by TOM ERDMANN JR., University of Washington

A MAD ROMANCE

I remember
how the south winds came
and slapped the palms
across the pane
of the second story window south.
I remember
a darkened room, the mouth
to the east, two windows,
the only light.
Through these the chanticleer,
rusted tight,
lied; his silent maddened tongue
was echoed
deep inside by a half-mad aunt.
She once glowed to speak of poison
in the cake
or snakes in the cellar. She'd take
precautions against pirates,
lions, worse;
or dash in circles,
almost hoarse,
to watch the chickens fly
or share the rooster's mad romance.

All care the doctors gave
brought her strong rebuttal.
Three times they returned her here
to the deepened puddle
of her memories:
her childhood home,
her single madness,
her old-maid home.
She never forgave
the winds inside
or those that screeched
on the window pane, and lied.
One night against the wind,
her gown a sail,
she wrenched away the lightning rods.

I remember
we were young then;
she, a member
of the family,
a race apart,
was dying
somehow against the wind,
always trying
to hold off death.
She failed.

That was yesterday;
today I stand
in the second story room
and hear her winds wail
with fantasies; scraps of gloom;
memories tied with string
to the poster bed;
dusts of hidden fears;
clothes, limp and dead.
These are legacies we yet divide
memories from the tomb
of her living suicide.

by VIRGINIA L. BECK, Sam Houston State College

MY CALIFORNIA POEM

Grandmother refused
to wear a bonnet.
Her light eyes
and dark skin
were extravagance
enough.

Thistles, their reds
and grays, parsley
and the firm boxing-
glove of the Opuntia
made a garden
peculiarly hers.

Ladies in Boston
may stare at the sea,
grow thick shrubbery
and marry men of letters;
it's all in their memoirs.

But no Western woman
ever nurtured
lilac attitudes.
It's the secret
of our life
in the desert.

by **RUTH HATCH, Scripps College, Calif.**

the campesina
         of asturias
             carrying
             a wicker basket
         on her head
has become
the whore
             in the streets
             of madrid
she wasn't beautiful
             in asturias
and she's no more so
                         here
her features
         are somehow
             still rough
             still she wears black
         to distinguish her
         from the earth
and in the usual
             cheap
             airless
                     hotel room
                 five flights up
                     cold running water &
                     plywood furnishings
thinking of the
         ingenious countryside
         of asturias
wishing
             it had been
                 where i was born
                 and could go back
                 to
but knowing
         that the days
             are filled with long hours

that the life
            is tough
                there
gives it
  boundaries and
        limits that a man
  of my growing up
  on the promises
                and
  the dreams
            of the city
cannot accept
like he cannot
        accept the springtime
    flowers
        just don't grow
        out of the wall
  and the tediousness
    as we search
        for familiarity
    and a place
        to be comfortable
has nothing
        to do
            with the seasons

by MARTIN NAKELL, Merrit College, Ore.

six soaring gulls
casually pulled down the heavens
with an effortless series
of wind-full winging undulations.

walked into the bathroom,
looked into my eyes.
suspected several spies
had dropped out of the skies.

two laughing lovers
ran sweet across
a morning meadow.
her loose hair blew.
bare feet through fresh dew.
three times he
wrestled her low
in the high greens
of spring.
she slightly resisted,
mainly smiling.
six birds sang.
two bells rang.

two trees kissed
against a cloud.
their joy was loud.
a hundred leaves applauded.
the wind nodded.
the same trees kissed again.
the earth began to spin.

by ROLF McEWEN, Claremont Theology School, Calif.

PICASSO'S PROFESSIONALS

in a Juarez plaza

      off the avenida 16 de septiembre

amidst the brilliance of

       gay pink
           dazzling yellow
     robust red
       and

                    moody purple
                                paper flowers

                    straw sombreros

                    emaciated woodcarvings

a chihuahuan homer hacks an ancient violin

Zapotec threadbare voltaire pounds dilapidated balsa
                                                    and
                                                      a

mexican machiavelli with three string bass

                                        tempts

                                passers-by

                                with

their reckless rendition of

                                elranchogrande

today

in

george bernard shaw's

tourist

theater

At the rosary for Don Pedro

                                who has left life at eighty-six

I offer prayers

        between daydreams

                hoping a sinner's prayers will matter

The widow philosophizes

            "Dios hace lo que Dios hace"

At the hospital

        Yolanda

          pretty Mexican nurse

between dreams

                assists a childbirth

by LEROY QUINTANA, University of New Mexico

MEURSAULT

The feet struggle
through bugs,
dung and dust.
The rubber Paris shoes
melt,
drag pebbles
down a road
rotting with Algerian apples.
At the dawn
of each second
strips of heat

199

burn down
the black suit's
white neck,
together carrying
the box symbol
to the ritualized ditch.
A dozen handkerchiefs
swat sweat drops,
comb steam from blue
eyes or blind.
Fat hips of water
bruise the earth's
parched face,
fracturing under
the Sun's heavy hammer.
Beyond, a fence
where Arab shadows wait.

by STEWART LINDH, Reed College, Ore.

NEAR "THE DANCERS" TEMPLE

I

old indian
      childless
      now
does not speak.
eyes brown and thick watch
dawn show a gnarled smile
east
           another turn
and rain slaps
tiles
shivering his reflection.
on the mountain
                    high
other lurkers
           wait, listen
in the rain.

chac whispers wet secrets
washes
browned jade eyes
of lean dog's
wait
under shadows of church stone pillars;
mother indians
sit
      cross-legged, laughing
and hawk mangoes
to the empty square. others
watch
on the mountain
listen for a return,
gods' breath old dust past.

II

in the tombs
skulls
harden
do not stir sculptured caves,
smile at thirst.

III

the "voice" is refuge:
  i need words, old man
but my tongue
is swollen and you refuse,
horde "the dancers' "
        step and leap,
the old feasting;

revery, bloody night's echoes
resound wordless
in your eyes.

nevertheless, i wait,
eyes glaze,
seek signs,
reach back through blood,
fascinated
unspeakable
alone
among the watchers,
to smile
with thirst.

by **D. J. PJERROU, San Francisco State College**

STATE OF THE UNION NOV. 1968

a weehour san francisco
doctor in a goodwill suit
bends over the rear end
of a beatup plymouth rocket.
reaching in his pocket
he pulls out a hip flask
& tipples whiskey
into the gas tank.

redwhiteblue streamers
hang in the cape kennedy
operating pad like
limp crepe testicles.
a male nurse squirts
his syringe in the ear
of a nude plastic corpse
& proposes an agnews toast.

thru the closed circuit window
two meat wagons with
a stripe down their pants
slink off with some captive blacks.

a squadron of blueshirts charge
porcupine clubs bristling
crowds pushed in a poke
bricabrac catcalls sirens

the sun
    the Sun kickS over
         half-gaSSed
   & SputterS towardS the inaugural
         ballS
     SparkS
      flying out
   reckleSS

by ART BONTEMPI, San Francisco State College

AFTER DRINKING ALL NIGHT WITH ARNTSON

(When we see who can write the best poem)

This morning our poems ripen
under glasses, and bottles, and filter-tipped
ashtrays, hiding the alcoholic
assumptions of our images.

I drink cold orange juice
and re-read the poems. In another room,
Arntson dreams himself into a grain elevator
and plots his escape through the brown,
infected wheat of a hangover.

He will stay here all day,
smothering the hours until darkness
and his smooth hands return.
I cannot tell him his poem was better,
so I silently watch him; borrowing
his paper, his socks, his images,
and returning these with the memory
I ink into his mind.

by ROBERT KUNTZ, San Diego State College

JEALOUSY:

I saw their shadows
    running down the bluff,
        falling like leaves
            into the grass.

My feet were cold
    in the moisture of autumn
        while they ran past
            darkening walls of knotted trees.

And memories . . .
    Faded traces of shaded places . . .
        Feeling degraded.

by JOHN CALLICUTT, Whittier College, Calif.

ONE DAY

Jack stood up and walked away
One day, and never came back
To take his place in line.
That was fine; since I sat behind him
You see, and was moved up one
Seat because he was gone.
His desk was walnut and better than mine,
And his chair was softer too.
It was real leather, and felt . . .
felt smooth and cool, like
A running stream with trees standing around;
I liked it. I sat and stared
At the swirling walnut grain
That wove this way and that and then back again.
I dreamed, sitting there. I did
No work and my boss said I could

204

Be replaced by a two-by-four foot computer
Who works for six cents of electricity a day;
So shape up, or I would starve and
Be useless the rest of my life.
But I didn't believe him at all.
I stood up and walked away
One day, and never came back
(Just like Jack) to claim my place in line.

by JOHN F. MALEK II, Western Washington State College

THE GOD OF LOVE ASSUMES MODERN GUISE

(for Elizabeth R. Homann)

One summer day, walking down by the depot,
Drowsy and hung over, I decided to rest beneath
The oleanders and palm trees, hoping for a train
To pass to relieve the dulness of the weather.
But no trains came and the sun beat down
So relentlessly that to give up even that sketchy
Shade seemed unnecessarily laborious.
And truly, as old poets tell, I fell asleep and
Dreamt as follows:
                              I thought I saw the
Station master or second trick operator stroll
Toward me along the tracks. He saw me
And invited me to accompany him on an
Expedition on the railroad. We hefted his
Small, hand-propelled car onto the tracks
And, pumping vigorously, sped westward
Into the sun. Looking behind, I saw the
Clump of oleanders and palm trees recede
Into the dusty day and, looking forward,
The marshes and willow thickets come up to
Meet us. He said he was the God of Love.

He wanted to show me his country estate
Which was a little town to the south and west.
The principal citizens and lovers were the car dealers,
Followed in importance by the insurance salesmen who
Sold insurance on the cars. The main industries were
A slaughterhouse and a grain dryer, besides, of course,
The creation and education of children. Thus this
Spa of love resembled all the bowers of romance.

It had a railroad depot, too, but lacked
The oleanders and palm trees so familiar to me.
Somehow the love expressed in the town of the
God of Love lacked something also; I was
Never taken into their bosoms for one thing:
They seemed sufficiently satisfied with their own
Internal ecology of love, excluding strangers.

But it was only a dream and I don't suppose
The God of Love even to exist; hardly in the guise
Of a station master or second trick operator.
Still, we all know towns and cities like the town
Of the God; and the dream may actually
Be happening.

by HUGH MILLER, University of California

A BLUE-BLOOD

"Ah, Jess," he said.
"Ah, Jess," he said,
and mentioned ink
and cigarettes
and said their smell
is like her own.

He had come
three thousand miles
and happened in on
Jessie's place
and smelled the
ink and cigarettes.
"Ah, Jess," he said,
and sighed and left.

Jess heard he'd come
and left again.
She shrugged and blew
a thin blue line
of smoke along the air.

by **CYNTHIA TUELL, Pitzer College, Calif.**

THE NIGHT WATCH

This morning fields were fleeced
in fool's golden dandelions.
The spring roar increased.

Lying in bed. In night watch.

A poem came wild—
the smell of a rain soaked dog—
and became a child.

Three in bed. Covered with night.

You had knit my raveled sleeves
coming out at elbows.
Your Ingres-like hip heaved.

In sleep. A porcelain line.

The words cracked like fire
in an April field at night.
The howling dogs choired.

Alone. Inscribing the old words.

The wild strokes of Van Gogh,
desperate and ominous.
The sky black with crows.

A hushed fray. You turned in sleep.

The poem was lost
in children's midnight chatter.
A belated frost.

Strong tea. The window dark with fields.

I see the haloed moon
in my snow glazed raku bowl:
a yawning raccoon.

by GAR BETHEL, Oklahoma University

BLACK TULIP

The dull light is red liquid.
Half-shut eyes, bursting bloodshot, nigger red.
High, heavy vibrations.
Close, hot cell of escape
Convicts of a slavetrader ship . . .

> Breathe deeply and
> Sleep; sweet aroma,
> Smoke seduced the mind.

> Exhale and awaken.
> (Money and power:
> Pot and peace).

Rhythm, man,
Do you got rhythm?
Blackness . . . (Africa:
Drum, dance, song) isn't, you see.

Power, sir?
How much power have you?
Whiteness . . . (Europe/America:
War, Sex, God (is, and it's a fact.
                    Love, love, love . . .
                    (Could but hate as always.)

Progress   Freedom
Money   Virtue
Ideal   Real   Material

Race equals Sex . . .
If you want a log cabin
Go chop down a tree. But
Lay the seed anew.

Ball and Chain
             (liberty, choice, marriage)
"Hide the dope; the Pigs are here."
"Is there really a Pope; does he really
Have a yellow cat?"

The dull, red light drowned!
In the humid, smoke-choked cell
The prisoners crashed.
But a candle (black tulip) still polluted the darkness.
Who's afraid of the dark, or is it the blackness?

"No suh, niggers ain't people, suh."
I've heard of limbo
It's heaven for any thing
Between black and white.

But God ain't white
He's grey
So go pray
And again recount your gold,
But close the door to the toilet.

"Did you see that nigger?
You mean that Negro?
A shadow, I suppose.
Let's go clean our guns again
And make love.
No, I've got to buy a new wallet."

The candle flickered and croaked
When finally relit an albino appeared.

"No suh, niggers ain't people."

But he did escape from the system
To be castrated in Mobile.

Help!
I would like to die
But there ain't no goddam heaven!
But my father always said . . .
What am I going to do, now?

by **RICHARD C. WILPITZ, California State College**

THE HOUSE ON THE BORDERLAND

We dragged the coal-charred children
from the wreckage;
The wind whipped through the twisted cage
of shrieking steel
and splintered glass,
Three men produced the funeral mass
that began and ended
without repose;

210

the waiter then recited prose,
(as we dragged the wilted tulips
from their soon lamented stand),
Travelling light
on a summer night
to the house on the borderland.

We pounded our sun-swelled snares
from the gravestone;
Ten bugles belched a solemn moan
in harmony
with the morning crowd,
The parson wore a sequined shroud,
and touched the frozen faces
with a coal-scarred thumb;
the waiter praised the deaf and dumb,
(as we pounded the pine package
to the soon redeeming sand),
Travelling light
on a summer night
to the house on the borderland.

We raised the bleached-bare banners
from the wreckage;
The wind raced in a willful rage
from clouds that wept
with unseen eyes,
The digger found his paradise
in a barbored hymn
of crumpled glee;
the waiter polished up the fee,
(as we raised our heads in mourning,
accompanied by the band),
Travelling light
on a summer night
to the house on the borderland.

by C. RICHARD RYAN, Northern Arizona University

MOURNING CLOAK

A violet
blue butterfly
went dancing
in the flutter
of an evening sky.
would
you had looked.

shadowy streaks
of up and down
silhouettes
blue and fadding
slant long and lovely
still
the dark wings.

never will be
nearly empty
of such nights—
silk and silence
flutter beautiful.
would
you had looked.

by GARY BREWER, Sonoma State College, Calif.

INDICTMENT

You who sit wondering
How John Smith—
    With steadfast, staring eyes
        And convenient credit cards—
            Can proclaim God dead
Should not wonder.

He, too, has felt
        The troubled shadows of time
           Mounting in homo's life
              And his response?
Buy out!

John has finally heard
        The result of man on man:
           Rats in children's cribs,
             The orphan song,
                Echoes of shot in the street,
                    And the unanswered cries for freedom
                  Creating a civil war.

We, too, have wondered
        If we could cry,
           If we could understand,
              If we could forgive . . . .
And John—as you have—we have wondered *often*
        How God could live.

                by DOLLY ROGERS, Whittier College, Calif.

ON SUFFICIENCY

In the morning of the day which was to be
sufficient for the job at hand,
the trees stretched out their fingers, frail
frames in which to catch the puzzle of the sky:
the welling wound which was the sun's blood dawn.
Below, the trees engaged the tide with rooting filaments
and stretched the rhythm slowly
to the synapse of the twigs, their tips:
from suckling womb they sailed their seeds to wind
and whispered to the troubled Thunder;

anticipating in the rising wind a restitution,
they felt its tremor roving on the morning
through the acquiescent grass, and then declined
their synthesis of light to bow before the judgment
of the earth-born sun.

The Thunder knew his ancient adversary, and he rose
and fled the sun's inferno, raging in the asphalt streets
of Dis, feeding on the city's furnace metal
as on the immolation of the amber grain.
And in the flaming dusk, once fore-named Ragnarok
by ones for whom the day became
sufficient for its evil, came the trembling Thunder
to his place, treading the heavy heat;
and to the smoke, the earth, the writhing trees
he spoke: "I summon the swelling sky
to touch once more the boiling seas,
to let the darkness soothe the Twilight's burns."
And he turned to savor the rain's taste
from the East where morning ever turns.

When the Sun rose again, on the after-morning
of the day which was sufficient
to ensure his never rising,
the Thunder groaned with expectation. Trees
raised leprous hands and palsied limbs to hope
to catch the Thunder's flashing hem, his scudding robe.
And as he walked he wept for those
who bore Apollo's witness, sons of Argos, Athens, Sparta,
those who when the earth was young,
investing dank and brooding forests with their mysteries,
assumed the gift for which Prometheus bled, then gazing deep
into his ring of blinding magic, found there the Saving Sun.
Faithful unto death were they, disciples, sons of heroes,
sand-footed men who stood at dawn, fingering swords
and searching omens in the flaring sky
                              above the seaward beaches

by RICHARD C. DAVIS, Pepperdine College, Calif.

RAINY NIGHT WALK

Cold rain pours its fingers over me,
The luminescent wavering of the moon pervades
My backmind and, an
Ethereal night shadow, I am of the fog's transparent
Substance.

The sound of my water muffled step pulsates
Gently in my senses and I am but another spirit of
The night underworld, a
Shifting unstable shape in the dreams of men.

by GREG CORLE, University of New Mexico

RED QUEENS IN A ROW HAVE THEIR TROUBLE TOO . . .

He went out and got the other kind of drunk today
i was afraid for his woman who stared blankly at his
stumbling trail . . . he faded three more shades at his
sobering experience and then faded three more . . and we
stay alone to avoid him in his stumbling fallen down
way of attacking you with his breath . . . we felt pity for
a long time but that changed along with his voice when
his ways became excusable only upon his death . . . lights
went out all over the world on my birth and they are
all only waiting to go on again . . .

series of serious men
have at odd times pointed and screamed
seeing horrible and terrible only diminished
really extant greater in mass and form . . .

215

and in the torn and disrespectful forms
of the end of afterwards (the one we search
        without hope)
the red queen resides caressing the collective
cock of mankind . . .

see . . . she wants the juice of our labor
so insertion or insurrection or whatever it is now
can with unerring erect arrows pierce her
and thereby make her new so she can die too . . .

the red queen rests preparing for the eternal
orgasm pleads from her lips falls aimlessly on me
and we give of us all of ourselves . . .
but the queen isn't happy collectively

passionately she wants not to be passionate
she disparages sex sexually waving her deformed cunt
she pleads with lizarded lips for a smooth
pair to release hers . . .

she's a nigger and she knows it and she hates it
our collective white to pink cock just ain't enough
so she stays in her pride alone . . .

        by TONY MATHEWS, Loyola University of Los Angeles

Sitting there at my desk
Staring at the February bulletin board—
The third grade.
Looking up at Miss Satterwhite as she
            pinned the paper hearts to the wall
            and winced as each pinpoint pierced
            its destiny.
Staring at the bloodied paper
Wondering whose hearts they were, laid before me,
            exposed to the ridiculing view of little children.

Watching after class as she
fixed her graying hair with
grayer hands
and gazed beyond the artwork
she prepared for our entertainment.
Self-humiliation.
Asking her why she was crying
Understanding nothing, yet somehow understanding
She, damp and smiling, replied "There are
no paper hearts; you, who are alone,
must know that. We are all alone,
and we
who are alone
are together.
It is the only tie that binds."
Walking out to the snow.
Crying, and not knowing why.

by KATHY SHELEY, University of Texas

REQUIEM FOR A BEAT

jack kerouac, hear me talking
i heard you die today,
it was a lonely sound, like wind acros sempty tracks
i heard your voice go down.
what train will carry you now,
your dead freight, and who should care anyway,
we have your books for what they're worth,
sal and dean don't need you, they have their own magic.

jack kerouac, i saw your picture today,
you have short dead hair, and a dead print face,
and when i looked at you,
all the whiskey situations of my life
rose to my throat and choked me.

the paper said you died of "gastric hemorrhaging,"
    does that mean the miles of road you traveled
finally caught up with you,
    and that corso, and ginsberg, and red mountain wine
took your brain, and like an old woman you finally gave up.

    jack kerouac, i hate you, i have no need for you,
you have polluted me, and a lot of my brothers too;
    you sent me with dean and sal, you took me by magic,
i've crossed so many lifetimes with you,
    i cry bitter with no tears coming when i think about it.
to new york, to denver, to frisco i went,
    stoned drunk i sat, between pages of a dream i lived,
and no one knew except me . . . and you.

    jack kerouac, i hurt, i want to die when i feel like this
i'm busted by phoney hipsters, who take me by force
    and don't care for my heart.
you have left me so alone now,
    i sat and tried to take you away,
tried to take those etched ideas from my head,
    but denver and railroads, and wheatfields in oklahoma,
and those long streches of road between here
    and wherever i'm going, still stay,
and i love although i'm lonely.

    jack kerouac, i was blind,
if i had only known you were lonely,
    perhaps i would have come;
but you died dead and lonely,
    and here i sit dead and lonely,
i could do without that brotherhood,
        lover.

by PETER MINNICK, Arizona State University

SANSARA

It is past midnight
I sit below the open hatch
Drinking hot tea under cold stars.
Moment of contentment;
Hum of wind through the rigging
Clang of halyards against masts
Bell sound
Hollow
Deep in skull
Resounding. . . .

by STEPHEN SCHWARTZMAN, San Francisco State College

PORTRAITS

They gave Jack a giant,
not maybe forever, but on loan
at their best minimal interest.
They gave Cassandra a recital
at twenty-two: she gave visions
without ambivalence.
From four to six, Snow White
put in her time and talents
at the local dwarf dwelling.
But people will eat apples.
And people will find a prince,
much like Jack.
Only Cassandra will be in her pumpkin.

by EUGENIE YARYAN, Pitzer College, Calif.

OF HOMOSEXUALS YEARNING IN
PUBLIC PAY TOILETS

I have read their scroll
and examined their art upon the walls.
They are a lost and broken people,
their exile is greater that Zion's,
and need, for them, is hidden
in a room no larger than a closet.

And yet, hordes of ads mill on the wall
like Friday shoppers. And perhaps, in answer
there is a flower rarer than our truth;
a tide in their desiring arms,
something so elusive that we could
not capture it for our collections.

by JAY CARON, Colorado State College

THE COURSE

You breathed morning in my childhood, stirred the listening
    leaves
to beckoning thresholds, porches of light-limbed song.
My ears course out the sound now, mute as one who grieves.

Now the notes are many, knobbed in ultra-frequencies
untuned to single silence, static signalled long.
You breathed morning in my childhood, stirred the listening
    leaves.

Are You bound in moonsoil testings, in returning laser beams?
Do we tube the vapor presence, push nitrogen along?
My ears course out the sound now, mute as one who grieves.

Chanting vespered rules of silence, robed in sack-cloth dreams,
voices choired quest. Midnight kept the psalm.
You breathed morning in my childhood, stirred the listening
      leaves.

Where is the lost crescendo, the bowing of the trees?
Do You last the token tinsel, the pulsing of the throng?
My ears course out the sound now, mute as one who grieves.

We've catalogued and vaulted, bounced fading frequencies.
Where is the muffled tomb, the forsaken matin psalm?
You breathed morning in my childhood, stirred the listening
      leaves.
My ears course out the sound now, mute as one who grieves.

by JACQUELINE TAESCHNER, University of Washington

HIKE

Rock's indulgence—seeking disturbance
rippled explosive silence

and the red orb nuclear
world rim twilight's
hour of the wolf

as the mountain's judgment
   speaking ash and sand
      cinder buildings
    sunsets large airframe
     framed wall.

by DAVID C. ADAMS, Oregon State University

THIS MORNING

My footprints
Refuse to remain empty.
Baptising themselves,
They fill with powdered clay
That flows like rosé wine.

Tomorrow is hog sticking day
Providing the dust settles.

And Bettyjean,
The hired hand's young girl
With green-stick legs,
Drags a pushbroom across the cement patio,
Using her left hand.

While the stones of Crowe Butte,
My mind's bread,
Crumble, littering with stubborn pieces,
The sandhills below,
Below this place where my blanket spreads.

by **RONALD MOORE**, San Francisco State College

A COFFEE BREAK

I

The cup design recalls victorian lace
and quiet talk,
walks in a conservatory;
faces through the leaves—
green lace veils.

222

II

Inside, the coffee gone, the drying grounds
form in patterns;
lace again,
or funny faces
through the roots of trees.

III

Coming musty from the empty cup,
the smell of moulding lace,
or fishing nets;
severe tin-type faces
through spider-web branches.

by **DENNIS J. WILLIAMS, University of Washington**

MORATORIUM, OCTOBER 15, 1969

Forlorn, sharp edged winds howl through angle-sheltered
eaves, driving from their cracks summer's helpless spiders.

The light patter of the leaden skies has turned to
perforated walls of water.

Rows of rivulets rush like tiny rivers down red-tiled roofs
carrying their loads of ruined muddy webs, distraught
spiders, and some summer's dead dust over the edge
where the raging wind sweeps the ordered waters into
a single shattered mass.

The din of the storm has changed to a steady, deafening
roar now;

And the reading of the list of dead goes on.

by **LLOYD HILL, Sonoma State College, Calif.**

THE I IN WE

We knew it was gone, but could not admit
The loss. It's too much like defeat to own
That what was once secure no longer is.
Lovers who had become strangers even more
Strange for their having once been close.

We wandered thru the vertically ribbed
Walls of the renovation in the place
Where our love was formed, grew, and where it dies.
We sought its resurrection, if only for
The comfort of having something known to hold.

As the summers' evening light grew less distinct
We found the places of our love
Then talked of other things. We went up
The contractor's ladder to the barren loft
Where love had made a formidable pair.

Side by side we sat on the boards, facing
Each other, but looking away. Feigning
Indifference, controlling emotion,
Each uncomfortable in the knowledge of
The other. Wanting now to deny it ever was.

"Let's go," I said, then down the ladder, thru
Vacant rooms, thru illusory walls
That can't contain, don't retain any longer.
Objectivity was a good mask for
Sentiment as we went, fearing the exit
More than the entrance.

by JIM NAUGHTON, University of Washington

THREE WORD THOUGHT PATTERNS
FOR THE DEAD

— 1 —

Let it not
    be said
        that
        we
        have
            worshiped
                the dead;

    but only that we
        remember those
            lately
                of this
                    world
            with grief.

— 2 —

We give thee the best
    of the beauty of our
        world,
    living flowers for dead men.

        Delirious,
            happy the
                dead men wandering
        at last in space, knowing
                at last
                    what it's like
            being at last at one
                with the ecstasy
                    of nothing.

We give thee the best
    of the beauty of our
        sorrow,
    living sorrow for dead men.

We choose
   to pave
      our paths to you
         with
   flowers
      and sorrow.

— 3 —

While you lie,
   not waiting,
      the minute quantities
         of your dust
         and your ashes
            in the wind
      draw the moisture
            from our eyes.

From you we have
      taken
      our lives
         gained
            the guilt
      of our presence
and give you, in return,
      our sorrow
         and the Earth's
            flowers.

by JIM DAVIS, Rocky Mountain College, Mont.

OUT AT NIGHT

I clambered out the window, hurt inside.
The moon, the trees had captured
And jailed within their branches, cold and stark.
And I walked

Past a shadowed house or two, some deserted lot
Collecting weeds of crowded living,
Desolate, but for that.
And I walked

And heard the voices warm inside
Admonishing the dark and laughing
Confidentially at the slightest rustle from outside
And I walked

And watched the deathly light that cities
Spread upon the sky
Where street lamps persuaded back the night.
And I walked

But could not help but whistle
When the night dogs barked at iron gates
As I silently walked past
Intruding in the dark.

by MARK WAGNER, Laverne College, Calif.

LANDSCAPE

rock waiting to be bleached
sun washed
shaped by ages of rolling sea
drifting shifting never ending

sand on the wind blowing
continental years
beyond sight but felt
endlessly on the deserts of a world
where rocks and sand control
and the wind continues everywhere

by JACK C. HOLMAN, University of Arizona

INTERSTICES

The way that blue smoke winds
    into the deepening air of a wintry afternoon
Stirs immemorial patterns in the heart; something
    from the shadows behind the hill
                interrupts
    the warmth of coffee in my bones
With an uneasy prevoyance . . .

The brain has no reply for the slow pang
    of feeling what it never knew . . .

                of hoar-frost and
                wan-struck incantation
                to moonlight;
                when the white rock
                tilts.

Something in the dregs of light across the field
    means four o'clock;
Beyond the warm room I am gone
    where faceless sky
        meets faceless snow;
              where together they dim.
The clock takes my ear, but I am
    fastened to the draining of the light.

This cold stone keeps the earth,
    and the stubble knows . . .

                at the rib of the
                hill the bone
                bares its seed;
                and the dark
                is like pure
                crystal.

What I have been told in cozy company
    does not apprehend
        the passing of moment into memory,
    does not (to my unuttered fear)
    still the darkening reach across the land.

The trail of a hearth-fire is nothing
　　　　to the stare of sky.
　　　　　　　　　In the vacant pause
　　　　between chimney and black pine,
Something is being kept from me . . .
　　　　　　　　　　　howls
　　　　　　　　　　　a bloom of star
　　　　　　　　　　　from the eyeless,
　　　　　　　　　　　frozen north,
　　　　　　　　　　　from the black-knarred
　　　　　　　　　　　earth.

Another twilight bends soundless into evening
More easily than I had thought possible.

Now lamplight wraps us in saffron
And its warmth soothes the old wound of chaos.

Night hangs blankly from the windowpane,
　　　　soon to be forgotten.

　　　　by ANITA HELLE, University of Puget Sound, Washington

　　　　Birds soar scripts of prophecy
　　　　And a million eyes of wandering tribes
　　　　seek the sun off Mount Tabor.
　　　　They return to scythe the ripened green
　　　　from the breast of Deborah's hills.

　　　　The sons toss grain to morning winds,
　　　　Flinging birds in unknown paths.
　　　　The winds return with voices
　　　　And a farmer stands alert
　　　　to catch an echo of the land.

　　　　　by RAMAH COMMANDAY, University of California

DIMENSIONS

We who stand in open summer doorways
Unchilled by lack of sleep, alert and still;
We who stand in this manner and this mood,
Watching a black tree shape itself to dawn,
Listening to humming crickets in the damp
Untrodden grass;
We know,
We hold
This moment in ourselves
And are removed as surely as the dim
And sleepy cricket chirping endlessly,
And are as still as blank wet leaves that hang
Motionless against approaching dawn.

We do not need the endless curving dawn
To light a way inside ourselves
In search of what we are.
We are what our empty hands hold.
We are what our clear eyes see.
Dawn moves.
We are eclipsed by time.
We know ourselves
In this still moment.

by **BETTY CLARE MOFFATT**, Texas Wesleyan College

THE INHABITANTS OF CAVES
(for Nancy)

Minding the wine vats.
Dusk assumes the impossible
dream of a bat, wings in low
and captures the woman
in her sleep. The body

stairs. Pillows of warmth descend
on a man's whisper.
His words are unborn.
A placenta
is full.

The bat is surfeit. Shadows
glide under his knuckles
and the creature is a ghost.
Stars sip his meat, the
bat grows.
Even the young moon
is visible in her purple breast.

by RICHARD TAYLOR, University of Arizona

The clouds were there in the morning,
Sent by a
Lordly yellow face with a wide grin.

The winds waltzed them across the sky.

Pale with joy,
they stopped
And rested among the light.

I won't wait for you in the
Darkness of earth
                    —I can see by your eyes
That you've escaped
                    and joined their elusive dance.

by BETSY CARROLL, Pitzer College, Calif.

DAY OF ATONEMENT

Section 31b of the tractate of
the Talmud known as Rosh Hashana

For forty years a futile *Yom Kippur,*
Since Why-hast-thou-forsaken-me's release
Usurped the bleats of sacrificial beasts
Upon the ridge that's skull-like in contour.
The priest, though doubtful, tries to reassure
The contrite as he ties the thread of fleece
Between the scapegoat's horns, but tears increase
The fear that rites like this cannot endure.
His sprinkling now performed, the priest returns.
The people blanch, the scarlet cord does not.
Without a word they drag themselves back home.
Sharply a trumpet blasts. The belly churns.
The Romans batter walls. The Jews are caught
Until Messiah's *Shofar* sounds *Sholom.*

by ROLLAND COBURN, California State College

ORGANUM OF SPRING

beneficence of God on April's ground
the somber clays grow restless and aware
dark sentient seeds expand
in silent kyrie, as deep in earth
the hidden waters rise
in adoration . . .
mute worms withdraw from light
leaving their manifestoes, credos in soil
pledged in humility . . .
green canticles compete, declaring
sanctus, and birds' antiphonies
return the agnus dei for adam's sin
as God walks
through incipient gardens.

by FAITH INGLE, Texas A & I University

"THIS ONE'S FOR YOU, REX"

Louis Armstrong said that
to the King of England
at a command performance
in 1932.

History does not record
what Rex replied. Poetry, however,
assumes he got off his high horse
and jived. That one's for you, Satch.

Everything is possible: the stunning heiress
proposes to the dwarf who sells oranges.
The moon barks at a serene white dog.
George Rex leads Dixielanders with his sceptre.

Poetry takes you by surprise
but not the surprise you thought:
like a birthday party
for the birthday cake.

by HOWARD LACHTMAN, University of the Pacific, Calif.

NO MORE

When the vagabond falls through the misty wall
    separating time from real life,
When he falls through the thin membrane into the
    lost world of sight and sound
Then he's lost to wander forever and no more,

When the white collared boy goes down in the damp
    dirty dungeon and he's searching for the
    black cat that isn't there
And he comes up screaming, "I found it, I found
    it, I found it" then he too is lost to
    wander no more.

When you're riding on your train of life and you
    reach the end of your line,
And the conductor's shouting, "Get off or you die!"
    and if you jump you will die anyway,

That's when you realize you are a vagabond,
    In mind, body, and soul no more. . . .

                  by BOB JOHNSON, Sam Houston University, Tex.

EPITHET

We are sensuous martyrs, infallible fools,
enigmas of genuine worth:
    glazed eyes staring out from empty heads
    lithe tongues clicking out amenable phonemes
spawning theories and
    notions and
    nonsense with the faultless
accuracy of
ticker-tape machines.
. . . resounding, rebounding didactic of
NOISE:
    uncomfortably eloquent,
    inaudibly safe.

There is your beauty and mine yet
we are bound to die (strangers)
excusing each other as having been
(simply too beautiful to touch).

                by JEANETTE HANSON, University of New Mexico

A NEW PLIGHT

A few sparsely spaced trees stand
    at the bottom of a rust-colored hill
while others have gathered together
    at its stony crest.
Near the zenith of this rolling green carpet
    stands one tree—alone, bleak, and brown.
Its finger-like branches beg for water
    and a place among the rest.

The green trees stare in mock silence
    and seem to whisper "die now,
So that we can take your place
    and the strength that you are draining from us."
But the brown tree stands alone, silent,
    and alive!

    by **JUDY BINDEL, Dominican College of San Rafael, Calif.**

CHILDREN AT A PLAYGROUND

1.

Given over to the earnestness,
The quiet deliberation of play and making
Great roads in the sand, the running games,
They pack their moments with intensity
And seem to sense the rising of dark clouds
With no idea of change, no difference;
They could just as well play in the rain.

2.

Some things we make timeless in our sight;
This ground and its devices in the storm
Stand like spectres of a separate world;
A swing still moves and makes a scraping sound,
The sandbox highway begins to lose its grains,
And in this haunted place the hush of rain
Conceals the echoes of those yet to come.

by TOM MAC MORRAN, University of Houston

LACRIMUS

Tears dot pages,
leaving spots of wrinkled paper
and crooked little rivulets
as they rush
down the page,
washing away the ink,
and leaving half-faded words,
and little salt deposits
like a miniature Bonneville Flats
for some bookworm to race his fingers across
at 10,000 a minute,
with 97% comprehension.

And a big sigh,
then nothing,
til the reservoir fills again.

by LARRY LARSON, Hastings College, Neb.

FOOTPRINTS

Spring rain that found
Compassion in summer ponds
Rests lonely in autumn puddles
Waiting for winter
While I in overcoat
Scan my time swept beach
Throw mad fists in deep pockets
To find the wadded hopes of
Sustained warmth
And heave them to a
Cold October sea

On the bluff above these sands
Into the wind an old man mutters
From an old coat then
Turning
Pulls his wrinkles back in a
Worn collar and
Trembles off the horizon
Leaving no doubt
As I stiffen in the wind
That the only footprints on
This beach
Are beneath my clattering feet
On the cold floor of an
Autumn Puddle

by **RICHARD L. BROCK, Orange Coast College, Calif.**

OCEANS ON THURSDAYS

And gentle walks
the aging morn
with swinging hips
arrested in mid-limp.

waves hang
as if they were
washed out the night
before after
a palsied neighbor
had eaten
all the starch.

Sand sat
with her skirt tucked
between her knees
on a hard backed
chair opposite
the minister.
I didn't itch
before I came.

by SHERYL KINDLE, Sonoma State College, Calif.

CORDELIA

Cordelia failed the test of Lear;
And he went mad among the rest,
Wandered through the storm within his brain
Til she returned and eased the pain.

His lungs are heaving as he waits,
With simple flowers on his back,
For just the softening of her stare,
Or one last breath; "Look there, look there!"
He kneels, her body in his arms;
A fragile death defining life
For clumsy Lear at center stage;
The dragon abject of his rage.

by KEITH R. MOUL, Western Washington State College

SNAKELINES IN THE RAIN

Wednesday threads paths through cellophane;
moisture, stripping her, whipping her without reprieve
contorts the world: brick blurs under water,
gnats scuttle across panes, stirring, whirring
in corners. Ideas, Bach in perfect pitch,
hum against glass, wreathe about each other; then
twist through cracks, off key,
becoming scarves on Autumn branches starved
for one sheer breath of wind.

Snakelines braid paths through sunlight as
companions to the bloated, listening worms
washed out on asphalt, soaking up the wet
until warmth cries, "Wait, hear the sounds of
soil below." Worms tense, then writhe in dryness.
Thursday's thoughts, gnats steam into focus. Lines
wrench on asphalt, sing
Autumn's song, giving breath to branches,
Come search for one that didn't die.

by SR. MIRIAM MICHAEL KENNEDY, OSF,
Marylhurst College, Ore.

NOTES FROM A BRIDGE

fingers tapdance over the bridge
of your guitar
tremble on stringed spans
wail like a gull caught
on the wind, unable to perch

fingers walk on foggy sundays
over the bridge
fret at hesitation
cry into silence
unable to perch on the wind

by CATHERINE WEISS, Dominican College of San Rafael, Calif.

239

THE WIND MUST DIE

Tonalia—ancient majestic mission green and growing
lies in spectrum between the purple walls of arroyo.
It is beyond the glowing lake that teems with fire.
Recorded tracks of travelers meander almost aimless
in the toasted sandy foreground of arid wilderness.
How many times they must have stopped to ask,
        "Can it be worth all this?"
Many pilgrims come here as dust to carve their
microscopic lines on the face of great cliffs.
They come to this arroyo on the wind and they go.
        But mostly,
                They come silent and are
                tossed this way and that
                to become part of things
                seen only from far away.
The wind that blows to Tonalia is a dry lonesome one,
a kind of wind that turns souls inside out to inspect.
All this it does coldly, without sound, without color.
        There in the desolate desert a man of Promise
        lost his way and died because of one seed
        of sand offered to him by the tempting wind.
At the rustic pine gate of Tonalia a gentle breeze
awaits the pilgrim to answer all questions with
whispering music, and life forever waves greetings
to the tired traveler come home to perfection.

by STEPHEN R. LARSON, Oregon State University

POEM

    I found a river bank
    I thought to be unknown
    By all but me
    I felt unique to have
    Come upon this shore

Where I vowed to
Sit and watch the day end
For all days to come
But I came to note
That this utopia of mine
Had known other flesh
The path well beaten
Hershey bar half eaten
Wrapper still clinging
To the semi sweetness
Initials imbedded in birch bark
Told that I was
Just another weary hiker
And I'm dying
From where I lie
I can see the river
Riding over rocks
Riding over me
Intimate death
Make me unique

I am a child east of the foam
Watching the sun
Burn a hole
In the sea
The night bird flies
The day bird dreams
Another sun
And two tides
Have passed
The sea flows to the sun
As I to my love
I stand a man
West of the foam
Burning a hole
In the sea

by LEROY SMITH, University of California

TO EMILY DICKENSON

I heard a saw buzz as I slept
Which, cutting deep the woody flesh,
Made shrill, excited murmurings
Like the sounds of a frenchman's guillotine.
And trickling past the noise I heard
The dying groans of a shredded plank
That bled small chips and dusty flakes
Into the pit of a fresh-dug bank.
The calloused hands of the carpenter
Condemned each board and unctioned it,
Then placed it on the tablesaw
And sliced its body, bit by bit.
They lie together silently,
Stacked so neat upon the mound;
The carpenter attaches each
And finished, puts them softly down.
We have one thing in common now,
You boards that firmly box me in,
We passed the saw's unearthly din
And lie in state beneath the ground.

by REX M. LAMBERT, Arizona State University

VERSE

Intangible,
     the season past,
days leaking between
    cupped hands, just as
rain water seeps
   through sucking soil
and is lost
    to a time of drought.

by LINDA J. LOVELL, University of Houston

THE PANEGYRIC

Siamese philosophers sing praise to
Winged virgins, the patron saints of
Christian soldiers smiles.

On the banks of eternal Nile the Asp
Of time stricks David's hand.
Prolific consummation of dogs.

The new world of Chicano falls
In foot time with Black, social
Unrest boundless man.

Gathering at the Philistines' door
Seamless minds coax the masochism
Of centuries.

Christian soldiers, Siamese philosophers,
Black Chicano White, cease to live and
Nero works; the proclivities of
Ensemble distress the mind.

by RODERICK T. TARRER, California State Polytechnic College

TRANSCENDENTAL INSTANTIATION

in bloody massacre
i slew one who cannot be because I am.
and, if I am substituting for messiah, My Commandments
are obscured in provincial colloquialisms—for I possess
no divinity degree.

but, using the Ethereal Nth Derivative,
the Snail i smashed (now He cannot be, too) divined Truth
from My Morning Yawns.

the End will come in Deafening Siren Screams
or Quiet Dreams.

let Us listen;
even with the burden of a Vampire's heritage surrounding Me,
I am no different than You.

Q. E. D.

by JAY FOGELMAN, University of Texas

LAERTES' SON

From France I came, to Denmark's distant shore
To see the graves, for nothing else was left
For duteous son to do—no vengeance meet,
No wergild to demand of killer's kin,
For all are dead. Felled by Fortune's arrows
They lie beneath the soil alike, and I
Have come to stand where then they stood and strained—
Like bowstrings taut to face the rushing foe—
To meet the strict demands of Honor's code
When father dies unshrived and killer lives.
    Old Fortinbras that then was young enough
To take the bleeding State and bind it up
Now stoops to touch the row of mossy stones
That bear the several names but common date
Of death, whose undiscovered bourn they share.
We kneel here, he and I, beside the stones
To give our thanks for Denmark's calmer days,
When blood revenge and foul incestuous sheets
No longer cause the conscience agony.
    But yet I feel (the king has felt as much)
A sense of loss that peace cannot repair,
A loss of men whose moral bones were bent
Beneath the swirling seas of worlds in flux
Yet stood to act and fall, unsure of why.

The world will long debate the tragic roles
Of Providence and Will and Fortune's hand
In felling these great souls of yesteryear,
Nor can I tell the merits of each man,
The just rewards he met beyond the grave;
But this I know: my father's final turn
Was to a better man than I have known.

by G. MUSACCHIO, California Baptist College

MAMMY

(for John Peter)

She was Pearl
with the cushion cocoa arms
to cradle him
in old songs,
unforgotten lore,
to the rhythm of tiny
cherry cheeked pumpings
at the nipples
of her dark perfect bosom.
Nestled in tightly,
the small blond skull
took music and
the nourishment in.

She was Pearl
who died
in his sixth year
leaving him with
the old songs,
unforgotten lore,
the music and
the nourishment.

245

Her death,
whispered to him by
the other woman
(with blond hair like his)
made him cry—
then sing.

by GEORGE BARLOW, California State College

THE PARK

you gave to me
tabernacles of blueberries
                              without stain
carried on the muzzles of dogs
with blackrimmed eyes and hair drawn
                                    lids
in the park where
            (prickly poppies are bought
            from sparetired skinned
            women
            calling from the otherwise or
                        otherinnocent
            sidewalks)
we walked . . .
aphid armed fetus
                  passed
in the full drinking horn of its mother
                              and
i remembered
when crowded with laughing
                  stains of red weed
hooked below
my nose
how your language-filled bodytongue

spilled
>> its juices on my earthdark
>>> body
below the park.

by ELIZABETH CRAIG, University of California

THE CHILLS OF RISING STORMS

Ceiling the sky in smouldering veils,
>> With snow flurries whirling outside,
The storm now as a beast bewails
>> Then cries out like a child.
Above our decaying thatch,
>> Suddenly a rustling sound emits
And as a lost soul of a hatch
>> Over the dormer-window flits.

Our crumbling miserable hut,
>> Full of sorrow and to dark,
What is it, my lady-of-the-old . . .
>> Compelled? For gone is the spark.
Either from the stormy-thunder
>> You, my friend are weary,
Or from a dream that drones under
>> A spinning wheel, time now to bury . . .

Let's drink, my good friend,
>> For our poor-seeds' choice,
Drink in anguish, here is a keg,
>> The hearts might again rejoice.
Sing me a song, how the blue-wrens
>> Quitely lived in far-away seas,
Sing me a song, how the maidens
>> Fetched water at sunrise in *peace*.

by HENRY SOBEL, University of Nevada

My Father was a Giant,
    a lumberjack with a red-and-black plaid
    coat. He could carry his axe and lunch
    pail and tin pants in one hand, and heist
    me atop his shoulder with the other.
    At the stump, not far from the back door,
    he set his load down a careful distance
    and cautioned me not to move.

                              He spit on his
    palms and hefted the axe, testing its arc,
    over and under, finally wheeling it, axled
    on air, straight to the stump to split
    a certain knot, or near. All around that knot
    the stump was feathered, textured as a carpet.

So my father came home from work, where,
for a while, he used to be a logging bucker
until the accident. He laid his foot open.
After that he had an almost office job, scaling.
I watched him once.

    He sprang, I suppose he thought nimble-footed,
    onto the flat-bed tongue, and poised there,
    ludicrous as a clown, handling the air for balance.
    He waved at me and smiled foolishly. A joke,
    his eyes pleaded. I nodded.

                            He pulled a measure
    from his hip pocket and six-inched it to its length
    across the furred base of each tapering log,
    scribbled some figures in his notebook and hammered
    a symbol onto the smoothest flat of the cut.

Back at the office, he kicked the chips loose
from his calk boots (they called them corks).
He didn't need them for his job, but everybody
in the woods wore corks, and so did he. He took
a ledger from his desk and entered his figures,
  and tallied it with his notebook. His job was done.

We rode home in a logging truck. He bragged
that he could hit a shoulder-high knothole
on our stump from twenty feet. And he could.
I sat proud.

Now my eyes are level with his. He wears
his lumberjacket because he's cold. He is pleased
when my children wheedle stories of whistle-punks
and timber-cruisers, of tree-topping and widow-makers,
of a bucking contest almost won.
                                          "Why, in my day,
I could throw an axe——." I don't listen. I know
it well. I watch his pale vein-ridged hands
whet and test his double-bitted axe to split
kindling wood for our fireplace.

                    by ROSE REYNOLDSON, University of Washington

BUMS IDLE

Bums idle in doorways,
Urchins float stick boats
In the gutters,
And lines of rags flutter
Trying to sail the dark tenements
To paradise lost;
But the slums don't play with the wind,
Forgotten rocks, ugly,
Eyes no longer see, sights unheeded:
Shattered glass,
Dog stools on the sidewalk,
Black brick,
Whores of the night,
The self-made man of glory,
Yankee dreams of log cabins,

249

Nothing . . .
But the stick boats of the imagination
Sailing on towards
The Hell of the dark sewer.

by DAVID F. BIRD, University of Puget Sound, Wash.

VOYAGE

Clouds drifted deranged above
The insane screeching of gulls
As we came upon him at last,
Lurching adrift between the sea walls
Rolling flash upon flash onto a sea
Of afternoon sun.

        After a calm,
He had returned again, promising
To remain among our potted green palms
And Dutch painted tea cups,
Forbearing, at last, that Columbus gaze.
But passing me, I saw it in his eyes—
Those wild, mad eyes—that the days
Had proved too much and he was seeing
Again some strange world, on a blue sea,
Far out in a void, far out
Of our vision, beckoning distantly.

In a moment he was off upon that sea,
With only its whistling wind wrack heard,
Our cries drowned to him in blinding waves
Of sunlight and the maddening screams of birds
As it took him; and he looked back once, long,
As if to check direction or balance differences,
And then was gone onto a blue sea,
Out of our world, all senses
Sailing madly off into the sun
For the last time.

by ROBERT DEES, University of California

WINTER SOLSTICE

I

His circuit turned
the king
hangs hooded
in the tree.
The trepanned eye
eclipses
in its winter socket.

II

The ark of seed
unwrinkles
in the soil,
winding its veins
rainward,
and the muted roots
mutter
in the winter earth.

III

From fathoms
in the loins
a dark river
blesses the flesh
and maddens
the tongue
with poems.

by GREGORY STEPHENSON, Arizona State University

CAIN

The bulk of him
moves heavily across the field,
trampling the earth's rich grasses,
the soil shuddering with dread.
His forehead clear, rigid,
radiant in submission
to immensity, the terrible
eyes, brilliant
as a cobra's or
the angel Samael's.
Seed of darkness,
cursed in the enormous time
of generations
and obdurate gods,
he pauses, hears once more
the commands of blood
and heaven,
hears the forests
and the earth singing
for the last time,
and bending to the young land,
grasps a jagged stone
and calls
his brother's name.

by MICHAEL PARRISH, Reed College, Ore.

HOMESICKNESS

(for Tricia)

She lives among steel and concrete spider webs
that shimmer in the heat glisten in the rain,
stick to your face and body
with the queer sensation of a shiver.

Pretty in pictures—with the proper light and color—
it invites, lures the bold and hungry full;
rejects, castrates the mild.
At night all the lights look as stars
only to see you look down.
A tree—there—is for initial carving
a dog to piss on.
The rain—there—doesn't smell clean.
Snow is grey, sooty with flakes of shit.
Looking up,
the sky is a jig-saw puzzle, jagged edges, no horizon.
With sounds of horns in Jericho
automobiles fart their smoke
mate with the factories belch
and reproduce coughing lungs, cesspool eyes.
The gentle people that live—there—push shove curse
smile—sometimes—
when they're stoned or drunk.
The running streams—there—flow over empty bottles cans
cigarette wrappers, soggy newspapers
occasionally a junkie.
Water that flows is clear
but thick with defecations and puke.
It smells—the freshness of three day used socks.

She looks west—out
between her strands;
surveys her forest—
leaves of neon and metal.
She sees the creatures that nest scurry crawl
devour the other creatures.

She looks west—out.
She shuts her eyes

And remembers a chipmunk skipping along a rotting log.

by PHILLIP DOYLE, University of New Mexico

SATURDAY, 2300 HOURS

midst the throes
of darkness
when private devils
dance in whirls
creating swirls
that fling you
to the night
men's voices echo in your mind
speaking with wooden tongues
that clack
like a wooden spoon
on a wooden bowl
the clacks
become more rapid and urgent
near the end
every tidbit
must be consumed
for when it all ends
and you are flung
once again
to
light
you must blink

by GEORGE T. NEWTON, Chaminade College of Honolulu

THREE-FINGER FREDDIE

Hark! The Herald
Examiner was deposited
in a neat, round pile
on my December step.
The Second Front Page
said America needs men like you,
like me.

Like me? Whoa!
Wrote them, called them,
even talked to them.
That's what I did.
When they acted, I took notice
and chopped off my trigger finger.

Yesterday, Memorial Day,
the Marine Corps took great pride
in awarding Crossed Magnolia Clusters
to their best left-handed marksmen.

by MICHAEL APPEL, St. Mary's College, Calif.

WEED

A soft cool rain warmed by a young spring sun
Sent tender roots down feeling in the dark
    Earth, where pushing up is harder.

I did not see you hiding, pining there
Until I felt your black pimple pushing
    Under tar, feet, me and others

Tamping down your all too natural burden
Until you burst your bondage blooming white
    For one eternal moment's freedom.

You were called weed to your fresh flower
Severed from your still reaching lower half
    By blind ignorance scuffling by.

by JEFFREY BRAY, Foothill College, Calif.

SEAHORSES

The dark wind pushed
   against her progress,
   and tugged at her torn
     thin clothes
Each step she took
   sank deep in the damp sand
   and tiny pebbles squeezed
     between her toes
     Her long, light hair
       blew softly about her shoulders
As she walked,
   a huge wave collapsed at her feet, and fell
   around her bare ankles
     She glanced at
     the nowhere of the ocean
       next to the sky
Her tears were hidden
   behind a veil
   of mist,
     and the blackened sky
     covered the pain
       she felt
She stooped
   and picked up a broken seashell
     and baptized it with her tears
     and squeezed it
     in her palm
She walked towards the water
   and gave herself to it
   and played with
     lovely seahorses in some
     dancing garden, and lived
       happily everafter.

by LEROY NEWTON, Linfield College, Ore.

EMILE—THE ARTIST

Gulls screech,
       Seals bark,
              He wakes with a start.

    Can't be still;
          Mind,
             Hands,
                Whole being restless.

    Overwhelmed.
          Must work.
Excitement of life
          Pulsates
             Within him.
Heart surges, almost bursting
With child-like innocence,
             Only Beauty exists in his world.

    Beauty is reality:
       Reality becomes beautiful.
    It is his Love.
With tenderness, passion
    He transforms
          rough, unshaped wood into a
             Sleek, soaring gull,
          coarse marble into a
             Magnificent black eagle,
          dull metal into a
             Bright-eyed owl.

by C. A. JACOBI, California State Polytechnic College

SHADES OF THE GIRAFFE

The Mazamba drum their logs
with wild incantations and erupting soul.
The fire casts the thousand warriors
feasting on the spirit of tomorrow's conflict
across the native wild.
With shadows long and leaping,
bodies filled with weeping,
children chained by mothers bound by babies crying,
women seething, heaving breasts,
men frothing, staring, whimpering revenge,
all join the swelling incantations.
Souls and bodies torn, complying,
grasping, clasping embered hopes,
tearing saneness from their beatings
and ever building to immense proportions
dreams of Gods and death!
Souls try to burst the shackling civilized
and walk the bondless clouds.

But dust suffocates the air
as dawn draws near with hazed refractions.
The sun has life and the fire has died,
one night has run its course,
and now their spirits are too spent for war

by STEVE CROWLEY, Wabash College, Wash.

VOICES IN RAIN: SHAPES OF THINGS

> Rapids of mind I seek to form
> before and beyond the passing.

Shades of everything,
wicked and warm.
Shadows wet as babies born,
wonder and warning.
Shadows fade . . .

> "Grandmother—a clock in the basement, a naked
>   shutter.
> Old and gray as the bible her tattered banner,
> she wore out her fingers in genesis hating adam—
> who traded the eternal lantern for eternal eve."

"This woman, first woman
of sea, and voyage and ship,
this clear wisdom in which light, pale and poised, sits.

"Oh, sweet jesu . . . Let me down,
lord let me down from this angry world."

"I speak of life as a world entering the world,
and each word is river . . . mountain . . . bridge.
each thought a nexus to the cleansing winds."

"My children are hungry . . . my breasts long dry bells
weakly tolling that wombs will not bloom and lips cease to
     wander another."

"As a pure shaft of steel, I see and reflect,
sorrow can never over reach compassion,
the flowers of the field mate without care."

"The path is blocked by a jungle of chaos
and the dead so deep are not beautiful . . .
The children are burning up among mobs of delusion
into smaller and smaller fragments of song.

Nothing can be held anymore.
Nothing can grow without woman.
The trees are dying."

"Give sun—
       something to say to the glad woman
       reaching at the hard night . . .

Give woman—
       something said to the fat sun . . .
       —o fat sun exploding on many palms."

"My man ain't come back no more to my heart,
and thereain't no more tomorrows to harken my soul,
because my need been swept away in the storm. . . ."

                         where rain soundlessly pours
                         and fills
                         the pockmarks of the earth,
                         everything open, every human being,
                         with silence.

"In memory of the antelope pierced betwixt dreams by a freezing
       flame."

"In memory of the everlasting recurrence of innocence as praxis."

"In memory, I become a folding thing
swung on a high swing
above the laughing leopards."

The endless summer and the endless winter
of hands that can barely hold to the pendulum of hope.

Man, the apocalyptic angel, condemned to be apostle of the rains
that fill every open thing . . .

    "My man . . ."

           "My child . . ."

"Oh sweet jesu let me lie in the cool rain . . ."

"We are sailing higher and higher into the rain,
up into the lizard light of rain,
—with the years tumbling against each other,
roaring and vomiting,
leaping back
and beating their hoary chests
to the tune of breaking waves.

For there is prophecy . . . that the wings of the lion shall
spread full in the rain.
For there is prophecy . . . of memory and hope,
of a suckling of the shades."

by CHRISTOPHER SHATZ, University of California

CHIEF JOSEPH, NEZ PERCE

Never reaching the promised land,
The fugitive chief
Sits in a corner of the prison car,
Chained to his warriors,
A featherless hawk in exile.

Seeing out the window
Geese rising like lost moons,
He knows more men died
By snow blizzard
Than by cavalry shot.

Still his father's dream
Of blue pines with black elk
Flashes in eyes
That chase the raven
Who croaks like a mocking cricket.

The old chief
Fought to break the cycle
Of cold weather and disease
His people swallowed and breathed
In the unfamiliar land.

This train rattles like dirt in his teeth,
Straw in his eyes.
Looking down into his prayer beads,
He sees the future,
A spiral of red-forest dust

That leaves his bones on the track,
His soul in the whistle.

by DUANE McGINNIS, University of Washington

SONNETS OF THE CITY

the kincott building

Rising out of Faulkner's sureties
Of old land and even older orders
Where Ikkemotube whispered verities,
Is the Kincott empire's steel upbounding borders.
Unfinished, the structure awaits delivery
Into the sun where it will be as calm
As Bengy's placid awe and revery
At growing's pulse and his unwrinkled palm.
Yet Kincott buildings bear no humility
For they are sunk to rock twelve fathom deep,
And every level bespeaks their fertility
And windy time does not disturb their keep.
    Earth is part of every pride that climbs,
      And new is respective of antiquated times.

the grey-brick building

Empty, small, unpopulated walls;
Between the traffics of obscure alleyways,
A grey-brick building unending leans and falls
And stays unfallen all its tedious days.
But that it is old, it seems a virgin
Whose shyness anticipates no marriage bed
And does not think her womb will ever burgeon
Great with life beyond her maidenhead.
Lowly, she will keep her place below
The tumult of the towers in the wind
And tuck her well-kept heart within, while woe
Wears away the proud without amend.
    This vacant hall retains its innocence
    And stands when other strengths have fallen since.

the first baptist church

The pews are warm from Sunday's busy devotion,
But no song or voice, sermon or human sound
Echoes in the chambers of this empty ocean
Where life for six days will not be found.
Achilles is the kin-most member here
Who forsook the field to keep his honor pure,
As these have lost the cross to stay Christ near
And want no blood to drip while love endure.
Though these walls a majesty command,
Unshaped, they were quarried common stone;
And if they were not braced they could not stand,
And bleeding not they are not *Crucifixus'* bone.
    Like time, like tome, like rhyme, the church is earth,
    And loosing that, it has no immortal birth.

by DENNIS MATHIS, University of Dallas, Tex.

THE MARY

THE PROLOGUE:

> I SUFFER
> contusions of the spirit,
> couched elegantly
> in indelible ingenuity.

THE ACTION:

> Mary rany up:
> Special virgin of
> five forty-year old virgins
> with curving breasts
> and all the rest
> (all that's needed for holiness).
> Nevertheless,
> I need my father's friend.

THE CONTEMPLATION:

> Moon blue woman:
> Mary,
> whose blurb
> depicts heaving breasts,
> the cambric hair
> the intricate kiss
> of Don Juan, John Doe,
> and who knows,
> maybe you,
> (I need my mother's lover)
> for it is a qualitative kiss
> quite apart from this world.
> Blessed are those who make bliss.
> kiss me,
> while computing
> your binary concepts:
> I'm seeing double.

The single (1) image
has devised two (2) wings,
    lives in different tracts,
        and fakes at different speeds.
Deal in facts, Love!

Over her,
white grafiti
of a men's
room
spread antiseptically
into a sheet
to conceal Mary
and the male genius
who feeds her
the lotus flower
of Evil eden.

    In the next century
    a butterfly,
        encased in amber,
            will call itself ingenuity
    and will unfold with caution
            its wet wings:

THE RESURRECTION.

by JAMES BURGETT, Berea College, Ky.

FOR LEE GRANT

Age 10

We sunk live fists, dead center
into rotting stumps, tore scrambling
down splayed ravines, war-whooping
and death-dealing to the widow-makers
lining the mulchy fern-decked

Land was sweet to our thrusting hands
circumspecting toadstools, ravaging the juice
berries that wove in the secret secluded
hideouts that we knew and made into
Captain Midnight strongholds, sending fern
spears against sudden onslaughts by gangly
screaming girls, axe-handed with nettle bunches.

At the top of an alder, dizzying from the height,
you rocked and sent me toppled to the depths below.

Age 14

We knew Larry the Lord of Tastee Freeze,
resplendent in white sheeted robe, bestowing
cigarettes to adoring acolytes who, droop-panted
slunk to the tune of Be-Bop- a-Lulu,
got tree-high on two frothy

Bears and birds were lost in the quest
for ankle-skirted, soft-sweatered girls
who offered mystery for anxiety at dances,
where, adoringly beamed on by Mr. Mudge,
we offered praise to the school mongoloid
and received a blank look, further asked
the local wall fixture for a dance and were refused.

On the beach, in swirling light,
you threw a blunt bone knife to my temple.

Age 20

Less even pennies, we styed in a
fisher-flower sacked, booze-bottle
stacked room, saw Mad Minugh
come, Africa Watusiing into our
Bolero-chanting room, singing of

Motorcycles sang to our sensation-raping
minds as we, rummaging a thin down, throbbed
48 hours straight to frigidly arrive
at the floor heated relief of Stevens
Pass where, after inhaling two burning
fifths, we greeted the goggle-eyed
rest-bound tourist with a naked ballad.

At twilight, in fast motion until the
impact, you sent us scraping over skinned concrete.

Age 23

With the Muse of Olympia and Gallo
furring our tongues, we moaned mad
verse to the insensitive tape recorder,
made a boiling brothel of Joe's trailer
with sultry, poetry-before-bed broads-

Sirens of the past called in that time,
slipping down the clay bank to the
kegged confusion party on the outskirts
of that wood we once knew, where
filled with buzzing drink, we crawled
back to the height and wandered through
the black woods, smelling pine and feeling 10.

Four years later, dead in San Francisco, you
light a forgotten trail, half nettle, half berry.

by BOB McALLISTER, University of Washington

ACKNOWLEDGMENT

We are deeply grateful for the help of the awards committee, faculty advisors, editors of student publications and these friends who urged and aided the launching of Laureate:

Marshall Buckalew, *President*
Morris Harvey College

Cordas C. Burnett, *President*
Bethany Bible College

Richard L. Capwell, *Dean*
East Carolina University

Sister M. M. Carbonell, *President*
College of the Sacred Heart
Santurce, Puerto Rico

James G. Harlow, *President*
West Virginia University

Richard C. Jones, *President*
State University College
Cortland, New York

Herman C. Kissiah, *Dean of Students*
Lafayette College

Arthur Knight
  Director of Creative Writing
California State College

Richard Linder
Department of English
Orange Coast College
Costa Mesa, California

Theodore L. Lowe, *Dean of Faculty*
Onondaga Community College

E. H. Munn, *Associate Dean*
Hillsdale College

J. James Redman
Bliss College
Columbus, Ohio

D. Paul Rich
  Director, Public Information
Tufts University

George W. Starcher, *President*
University of North Dakota

Stanley Stewart, *Chairman*
Department of English
University of California

Edmund J. Thomas
  Chairman, Division of Humanities
Niagara County Community College

Gerald Thorson, *Chairman*
Department of English
Saint Olaf College

F. Joachim Weyl, *Acting President*
Hunter College